GW01402884

BREAKTHROUGHS
AND BEYOND

7 Laws of Success for Aspiring
Entrepreneurs and Start-Ups

DR. RAJNI AGGARWAL

**A Woman's Entrepreneurial Journey:
Quest to Scaling up a Business
and Mastering Growth**

**Includes 8 Inspiring Interviews
of Women Achievers**

To all the courageous souls, passionate entrepreneurs, dreamers and the women who dare to take the pathway of economic empowerment in the world of business and envision a future of financial freedom and purpose.

May this knowledge inspire and support your pursuit of economic independence and success.

'Breakthroughs and Beyond' has come at a time when the entrepreneurial landscape is evolving rapidly and serves as a valuable resource to provide guidance on overcoming challenges, building resilience and seizing new opportunities. It offers a comprehensive roadmap for aspiring entrepreneurs navigating the complexities of business universe.

I commend your blend of practical wisdom with motivational anecdotes, making this book highly insightful and inspirational for anyone looking to make a meaningful impact on their entrepreneurial journey.

I'm confident this book will empower countless entrepreneurs with the tools they need to succeed. I wholeheartedly recommend this read to entrepreneurs and business leaders seeking to drive positive change.

– Ms. Mercy Epao
Joint Secretary, Government of India,
Ministry of Micro, Small and Medium Enterprises (MSME)

Dr. Aggarwal's vivid journey towards financial independence reveals the bureaucratic and social hurdles women face. Her story uniquely combines generational wisdom with insights into the business world, underscoring India's economic progress. This book is a testament to her determination and innovation and brings timeless insights, making it a compelling read for all those who are seeking strategies to align with their vision paving a path for their entrepreneurial journey

– Lata Singh
Partner, IBM Consulting

Contents

Prologue.. 9

Introduction 13

Chapter 1   Finding Myself..25

Chapter 2   Alice in Business Land... 48

Chapter 3   Gearing for Success 74

Chapter 4   Global Stage - A Way Forward 89

Chapter 5   The Art of Fundraising 116

Chapter 6   Networking: Become the Power Connector...........156

Chapter 7   Being Yourself - 'Not a Quitter' 180

This is the Beginning.. 205

References... 209

Acknowledgments 211

About the Author 213

Let's Connect... 215

Prologue

"Small beginnings are the launching pad to great endings."

- Joyce Meyer

"What management expertise do you have?" This question struck me like a thunderbolt when I approached a bank for a loan in the 1980s to start an electronic unit for manufacturing TVs and components. The Senior General Manager of a renowned bank and his other two colleagues in their chamber quizzed me and looked at me expectantly.

Charged with immense passion and unwavering zeal, I approached the bankers with high expectations, eager to secure the necessary loan and limits for my ambitious project. However, as the question about my management expertise hung in the air, a sudden wave of uncertainty enveloped me. Despite my resolute determination, I locked horns with self-doubt, questioning whether I had the knowledge and skills to answer that question.

At that moment, I found myself momentarily pausing—not out of a lack of confidence in my knowledge but driven by a desire to present, not just the right answer, but the one that was perfectly attuned to the gravity of the occasion. The pressing need to secure funding for my business propelled me to think on my feet, necessitating a swift and precise articulation of my managerial capabilities.

The episode spotlighted the disheartening reality of gender disparities in the business world. The unequal challenges faced by women in securing funding and sponsorship, coupled with the additional scrutiny encountered at every stage, starkly contrast the often smoother path navigated by their male counterparts.

Many women, seeking a balance between work and life along with the pursuit of economic independence, transition from corporate roles to entrepreneurship. However, even in the entrepreneurial realm, the struggle persists. The road to leadership positions is paved with obstacles for women, demanding an extra layer of resilience and effort. It is a scenario where merit does not always speak for itself, and women find themselves having to work doubly hard to shatter those glass ceilings.

The observation from McKinney's 2011 report adds another layer to this challenge, underscoring the disparity in promotion criteria. While men often benefit from being assessed based on their potential, women are judged based on their past performances. This not only perpetuates gender biases but also places an additional burden on women to constantly prove themselves, hindering their professional growth.

Addressing these systemic issues is cardinal for a more inclusive and equitable business environment. Recognizing and valuing the potential and achievements of women, both in entrepreneurship and corporate leadership, is not just a matter of fairness but also a strategic move toward building more diverse and successful businesses.

At the onset of my voyage as a first-generation woman entrepreneur, I came eyeball-to-eyeball with obstacles at every turn. These prevailed on both the home front and in the business domain. The initial challenge of securing funds to kick-start a business is a common struggle, with many women finding themselves in a situation where the path forward is hazy. Women, in increasing numbers, are facing this situation and often feel lost, in the absence of clarity as to where to begin.

According to the Boston Consulting Company's survey findings, gender disparities are highly visible and stem from socioeconomic, legal, and cultural norms and practices. Gender disparities can manifest in various aspects, including pay gaps, representation in leadership positions, access to opportunities, and workplace biases. These disparities often reflect deep-rooted societal norms, stereotypes, and systemic barriers that hinder women's progress and limit their full potential.

In 1982, when I started my business, the concept of women entrepreneurs was relatively unfamiliar to me. It was only upon my association with the National Alliance of Young Entrepreneurs (NAYE) that I met with a rare number of women who were establishing their companies or had recently joined their family's businesses. These encounters occurred during the NAYE meetings. However, I came to realize that these gatherings served as catalysts for enthusiasm, positivity, and, most notably, networking opportunities. I greatly benefited from the knowledge and experiences I gained through my involvement with this organization. As women, our reasons for joining such clubs differ from those seeking leisurely social gatherings with friends.

Our responsibilities as mothers and wives often necessitate our return home after sunset. Even when family obligations are not a factor, our natural inclination is to return to our nests. When I launched my first trading venture, my initial goal was to grow and generate profits. However, I was uncertain about the extent to which I could expand my business and how to make it truly profitable. Recognizing the need for a different skill set and access to capital, I understood that seeking the guidance of experts, bankers, and peers was essential to effectively manage all aspects of the business as its CEO and ensure its profitability.

Looking back, I earnestly wish that when I stepped into the business world, there were visible women role models whom I could learn from. While I was aware of a handful of successful women entrepreneurs, their stories were seldom highlighted in the media, and accessing them for advice was challenging in those days. In a later section, we shall leaf through the historical progress of the business ecosystem in India and how women entrepreneurs gradually became a part of it, despite pronounced gender disparities.

Introduction

" **B**reakthroughs and Beyond" is a sincere effort to hold up a mirror, providing you with the valuable mindset and skills required to propel your business toward unprecedented success. I stand before you as a woman entrepreneur, but my path to this point has been anything but straightforward. It is a tale woven with threads of perseverance, resourcefulness, and an unyielding belief in the power of self. This book is my attempt to capture the essence of that journey, to distill the wisdom gained from my experiences, and to share the lessons learned along the way.

In the domain of entrepreneurship, there exists an exhilarating dance between dreams and realities, between ambition and adversity. It is a world where the fearless take risks, where passion fuels innovation, and where the unwavering determination of individuals can shape their destinies. This is the narrative of my journey—an odyssey through the trials and triumphs of a woman navigating the unpredictable waters of business.

From the earliest moments of my life, I yearned to create, to build something that would transcend the confines of my imagination. I had dreams that stretched far beyond the narrow horizons of societal expectations, dreaming of a life where I could shape my destiny and make a meaningful impact on the world.

But dreams, as we know, are only the starting point. They provide the spark, the initial motivation to step into the unknown. The true test lies in the tenacity to weather the storms that inevitably follow—the setbacks, the doubts, and the seemingly insurmountable challenges that lie in wait.

In the chapters that follow, I will recount the pivotal moments that shaped my entrepreneurial spirit, the trials that threatened to extinguish the flame within me, and the victories that brought me closer to realizing my purpose.

Each chapter, in one way or another, reveals a facet of my journey, offering insights into the inner workings of a woman striving to leave her mark on the world of business.

The first chapter, '*Finding Myself*' walks through the arena of ideation, determination, and exploration. It narrates how a small spark within me transformed into a thriving enterprise.

In the following chapter, '*Alice in Business Land*' I share my experiences of turning failures into stepping stones in the business world. This chapter emphasizes the role of marketing as the lifeblood of any business, along with aspects of customer acquisition and satisfaction. Drawing from my own experiences, I emphasize the importance of entrepreneurial mindset, challenges, risk management and narrative on limiting beliefs

The third chapter, '*Gearing for Success*' is all about scaling up, leveraging strengths, understanding market trends, and managing competition and change effectively.

Moving on to the fourth chapter, '*Purpose for Bigger Plunge – A Way Forward*' we explore the intricacies of expanding beyond local markets and seizing international trade opportunities. I share the challenges and rewards of entering global markets and provide strategies for building an international network to drive business growth.

In the following chapter, '*Money Game*' I discuss a vital piece of the puzzle- securing funding, and share the lessons learned and strategies employed in my quest for financial support. From bootstrapping to venture capital, I explore the different avenues available to women entrepreneurs and shed light on how to navigate the funding landscape effectively.

Next, we discuss one of the most critical elements in any business scenario: '*Networking, Become the Power Connector*'. I share my experiences and tools for creating winning strategies for networking, time management and scheduling to get the most out of oneself, digital platforms, and understanding the ever-evolving marketing landscape to create a competitive advantage.

The seventh and final chapter, *'Being Yourself - Not a Quitter'* addresses the challenge of achieving work-life balance, a daunting hurdle for entrepreneurs, especially women. I quote my experiences and strategies for finding harmony, nurturing personal relationships, and prioritizing self-care while pursuing ambitious entrepreneurial goals.

Each chapter serves as a purposeful stepping stone highlighting the *7 Laws of Success,* laying the foundation for aspiring female entrepreneurs—a series of imprints to guide you through the journey of your entrepreneurial adventure.

This literary composition is a symphony where each woman's narrative adds a distinctive note, harmonizing into a melodious arrangement resonating with the soul of feminine leadership. A symbolic torchbearer, the book emits a guiding light, illuminating the way for women not only to endure but to flourish in the entrepreneurial expanse—a promise akin to the radiant sunrise heralding a day brimming with untold possibilities.

The Progress and Ambience for Women

During and after India's independence in 1947, women's active participation in public life was relatively uncommon across all levels. Nevertheless, there were iconic women like Kamla Devi Chattopadhyay, Sucheta Kriplani, and Durgabai Deshmukh who made remarkable contributions to various social enterprises. Gandhi Ji was the prime mover and supporter. Within the Congress party, under his leadership, he encouraged and inspired women to actively engage in the struggle for India's freedom.

I remember my mother wearing a white saree with a blue border when the Congress Party celebrated its victory all over the country. We were in Indore at that time. Gandhi Ji was enthused and influenced to bring women out of the kitchen and struggle for social reforms and independence. It was a dichotomy that even though Gandhi Ji actively encouraged women's participation in public life by saying things like "a woman is the companion of man, gifted with equal mental capacities, she has the right to participate in all the activities of man..." He also shared, "I don't believe in women working for a living or undertaking commercial enterprise."

During that era, it was a rare occurrence to find women independently managing businesses, engaging in trade, or participating in manufacturing activities. This was not because women were perceived as incapable of assuming leadership roles, but rather, it was a prevailing belief that women should confine themselves to different occupations. Societal norms dictated that activities aligned with culture and tradition, such as art, craft, music, and teaching, were deemed suitable and honorable for women. In contrast, men were expected to handle financial matters. As a result, from a young age, the upbringing and education of girls in their homes often left them lacking the skills and confidence required to navigate the challenges of the world beyond their domestic sphere.

All over India, barring a few North East States, it was a strongly patriarchal society. The dowry system prioritized a woman's social position in her marital family, followed by her natal family, aligning the interests of daughters with fathers and sons with fathers. Decade after decade, this practice indeed reinforced the idea and to some extent continues to do so, that a woman's worth is tied to the material resources she brings into her marital family, rather than valuing her as an individual with her own agency and identity.

The slow process of liberalization took a few decades despite the Government's initiative of economic liberalization since Independence. The macro situation was dramatically different at the dawn of Independence. The general expectation was to create conditions increasingly more comfortable for individuals to start a new enterprise.

On my first visit to the United States in 1982, the process of registering a company was quite friendly and straightforward. The systems were efficiently organized, and they provided a smooth pathway for setting up and launching a company, even for a foreigner like me.

I have witnessed discouraging incidents while advocating for an equal place for women in the business world. In 1985, a woman relocated from South Africa to India and established her business in Delhi. During her experiences in our country, she highlighted a fundamental issue in numerous meetings and conferences – the need for women's restrooms at major markets and bus stops. Sadly, in response to this demand, she faced sarcastic and insensitive remarks from male crowds. Neither the Delhi government nor anyone else showed sensitivity to this matter. In 1987, she returned to Africa deeply disheartened. Women, in general, silently endured such difficulties but lacked the confidence to insist that these problems should be addressed and given top priority. The ambiance sets the mood, character, quality, tone, and atmosphere of your business. During the period from 1975 to 1985, the business environment in India was far from entrepreneur-friendly. The bureaucratic structure was highly complex and cumbersome. The prevalence of the 'inspector raj' was deeply entrenched, and entrepreneurs lived in constant fear that any visit from an inspector would lead to unwarranted complications and an inevitable process of corruption.

The 73rd and 74th Constitutional Amendments in 1992introduced reservations for women in local governing bodies, marking a noticeable shift in power dynamics. This move placed women in positions of authority outside their homes. Many women across India who gained these roles through this reservation system faced criticism and were derogatorily labeled as 'quota candidates' because some men were resistant to this change. Nevertheless, this transformation was sparked by women assuming roles as Panchayat Presidents and Municipal Mayors. It was also facilitated by their active participation in trade fairs and exhibitions, where they confidently engagedwith government offices, initiating and attending meetings independently, raising issues of public interest and grievances, and seeking redress on their own terms.

There has been much debate about women's reservation in Parliament and State Assemblies; strong and negative sentiments against women's reservation have been expressed. One can see the differences across countries between the genders at the level of survival and sustenance, in decision-making and position of power. The UNDP's Human Development Reports 1995, 1996, and 1997 have contained a ranking of countries by a Gender Empowerment Measure (GEM). The GEM attempts to capture and rank international differences between men and women taking part in economic and political activities and participating in decision-making. The data indicates that in no country women were at an advantage; India was at the bottom of the list.

Many African and American countries ranked higher. Europe and the US ranked amongst the first four countries. Indian women constituted only 20.5% of professionals and technicians, 2.3% of administrators and managers, and held 7-8% of seats in Parliament, earning 29-26% of income share. This piece of information has spurred more initiatives, increasing the number of women decision-makers.

However, when women were enabled to function as equal partners and participants in the developmental process with reservations in the membership of local bodies, (the Eighth Plan) marked a definite shift from *"development to the empowerment"* *of women.**

The revolution started close to the 1990s, and many women started coming forward. The government also decided to recognize and define women's entrepreneurship. Awareness of women's economic participation had begun but with minimal visibility.

Today, India stands as one of the fastest-growing economies, and entrepreneurship has become a key component of the nation's economic landscape. Women entrepreneurs are making a remarkable impact in various segments of the economy. They represent approximately 20% of the total entrepreneur base in India, amounting to 8.05 million out of the total 58.5 million entrepreneurs. While the Micro, Small, and Medium Enterprises (MSME) sector holds immense potential, it remains predominantly male-dominated, particularly in the manufacturing sector. In contrast, the service sector is known for its continuous innovation, where individuals from the technology or sales sectors often introduce new ideas and products. With few exceptions, women entrepreneurs primarily focus on the service sector as their area of business activity. This is a brief background that conveys how women have crossed through this big gap of non-recognition to make their space in the men's world. While there is an increase in the number of women participating in businesses, the number of women managing businesses has increased globally. But still, women continue to face enormous obstacles that restrict the growth of their businesses. These obstacles include lack of capital, strict social constraints, limited time, skill, and mindset.

The Gap Prevails

Despite the growth in women entrepreneurs, very few have crossed the million-dollar mark, such as Kiran Majumdar of Biocon, Anu Aga of Thermax, and Mallika Srinivasan of Tractors and Farm Equipment. Why so? What are the barricades? The past decade has seen an explosion of women starting businesses. Today, free business tools are more readily available as compared to the times when I started a business. And emerging entrepreneurs want to solve problems in new ways.

Some women have successfully skyrocketed their companies from inception to million-dollar ventures within just a few years. Nevertheless, I have concerns about the future: where will women choose to initiate their businesses over the next five to seven years? Unfortunately, a marked number of women either operate small businesses or are compelled to close them down due to challenges like insufficient marketing expertise or financial constraints. My objective is to help women secure funding, dwell on innovative thinking, and address their challenges. I hold a deep passion for empowering more women to effectively develop their businesses.

In that spirit, I am keen and happy to share with you the stories of those women who worked from scratch and have successfully reached a million-dollar mark. Some of them are not featured in big business magazines, but they have proved themselves successful and they are powerful women. I have taken the stories of those women entrepreneurs who have worked between four to 10 years and have had a successful journey. Their entrepreneurial mountain hike is close to your journey and you can learn from every step of theirs. Some of them are not able to reach the first trek of the Himalayas Mountain of 10000 feet and stop there. This is what happens with most businesses. It is documented that 50 percent of all businesses fail within the first five years of operations, regardless of gender.

I have had the opportunity to connect with these incredible women. They come from diverse industries, including rubber, plastics, steel, sugar, beauty, education, women empowerment, paint, engineering, fashion, baking, and food. These women have traversed the challenging terrain of balancing motherhood, cultivating a thriving business culture, implementing innovative marketing tactics, taking bold initiatives, and contributing to their communities. Their resolute passion and love for their endeavors shine through in everything they do.

You will find none of them had any business background, nor had any formal degree in business, but each one had something special; they had the grit. To know about their inspiring story is a privilege. They can be your trailblazers if you are determined to make it big in life.

It is a matter of concern that women are twice as likely as men to close down their businesses due to a lack of skills and financial resources. Women often encounter challenges in expanding their operations and venturing into new markets. Scores of women entrepreneurs struggle with effective communication with bankers, lack the confidence to engage with potential investors, and are often unaware of the necessary compliance requirements. This issue is largely attributed to women not thinking big enough; they usually do not take substantial steps to gain financial knowledge, entrusting these matters to accountants, CAs, or their spouses. Women should recognize the potential and power within themselves. While someone else can help operate the chariot, it should be under her navigational direction. Only when she holds the reins, can she chart her course to the desired destination. Women must realize that having greater financial resources can solve many of their problems, such as hiring more staff, investing in marketing, focusing on business growth, and envisioning a larger-scale operation.

However, from the lens of my observation, men often secure more substantial funding, are more willing to take risks, and possess assets in their names. They tend to excel in building strong networks, resulting in the ownership of high-revenue businesses compared to women. Both men and women bump into failures in their entrepreneurial adventures, but women tend to face a greater number of setbacks. Therefore, how can we learn to raise more money, and do it our way? If you go through the interviews of top women industrialists and follow the steps I have mentioned in the book, you can learn to take a fast stride in making your business grow.

The onset of my entrepreneurship was in small-scale industry. At that time, the Government of India had two ministries; the Ministry of Small-Scale Industries, which covered cottage industry and small scale, and the Ministry of Industry, which covered medium and large scale. However, the definition of small-scale industries has changed 3-4 times since the time I started in the eighties. Now, it is known as the Ministry of MSME, which includes micro, small, medium, and enterprises (service sector) as well., which was not included earlier.

My heart is deeply committed to the cause of women's empowerment, and I am animated to handhold women to launch and expand their businesses. It was backbreaking for me, but through hard work and deep contemplation, I developed a strategy. This methodology is founded on three essential elements that can lead to success for women entrepreneurs: Entrepreneurship offers the potential for Income (**Money**), a sense of purpose and significance (**Meaning**), and the flexibility and freedom to adapt and move (**Mobility**).

For women, money is not about adding zeros and watching the numbers grow, as men might enjoy. Instead, it is about crafting a canvas of comfort—a comfortable life, quality education for their children, and creating a welcoming home. Women are more concerned about creating a meaningful and fulfilling picture rather than simply increasing numerical figures.

Therefore, finding meaning plays an instrumental role in women's lives. It also means her creative aspect to get to see the 'Light of the Day'. She loves to find the reasons or spend time on things that are taking away her comfort and time from her children. She loves to find meaning in her actions and their outcomes.

The concept of mobility, which is also the first preference for some entrepreneurs, is predominant. As an entrepreneur, you may find yourself working around the clock—whether it is 24 hours, 20 hours, or even, in some cases, 48 hours. However, what truly matters is which specific hours you choose and how you structure your daily workload. Having the freedom to select when and from where you work is a critical aspect, particularly for women.

Comparatively, when you contrast this with corporate careers, you will find that senior corporate executives do have some level of freedom. Nevertheless, their commitments are often as demanding as their seniority. Consequently, even though many corporate jobs offer a sense of security, women frequently undergo several career changes in their lifetime to find positions that better align with their desired lifestyles.

Most women think they do not want to be 'big' because it means more responsibilities, more commitments, overseeing a large size of staff, more money, and more responsibilities beyond the home. Owing to such hitches, despite having all the ingredients to grow, they cannot scale up their activity most of the time. But let us not forget, if we choose to be big, we can afford to engage a senior staff, more people to work with us, and have better management.

However, if one does not strive to go as big as opting for venture capital and higher revenues, one can increase the business to a better level than the current size of your business.

My trek as a first-generation woman entrepreneur has been unique. I have experienced several ebbs and flows; some left me shell-shocked, some added immensely to my treasure trove of learning, and some gave me cherished moments of jubilation. In essence, the journey has been truly spectacular! I believe we can do one thing to help all women entrepreneurs, which is to share our stories to help them grow faster and think big – and learn from each other's failures and successes.

As they say, knowledge becomes power only when it is shared; therefore, I did not want to limit my experiences to myself. And what could be a better way to share my voyage as an entrepreneur than penning it down? Apart from my memoir, the book is also turbo-powered with examples of highly inspiring, successful businesswomen who have shown courage, confidence, and conviction. These women have waded through all odds and swum bravely through the difficult channel of ups and downs of business with grace and fortitude.

I highly recommend that aspiring women entrepreneurs understand and adopt this approach. The insights shared in this book will serve as an immense source of motivation, inspiration, and resilience. This is a book for anyone who wants to leave their cushy 9-to-5 jobs that demand only target completion — jobs that are a source of stress 24X7. Their existence is always doubtful without the final marks.

This book is also for existing entrepreneurs, startups, and women planning to graduate from cottage to small, small to medium, and medium to large enterprises. There could not be one definition of success and happiness. Each entrepreneur must decide her own goals, values and dreams, and chart out the course of her life accordingly.

Throughout the pages of this book, my primary objective is to empower and ignite inspiration among women entrepreneurs.

I aim to offer tangible guidance and valuable perspectives in key areas, such as funding, marketing, export, networking, and work-life balance. My goal is to break down the barriers that often impede women from fully realizing their entrepreneurial potential and to encourage them to acknowledge their distinct strengths as they navigate the entrepreneurial terrain.

This book does not take the form of a memoir, nor am I a scholarly writer. While I have shared personal stories and the experiences of others, it is not merely a collection of success stories; it serves as a self-help guide aimed at providing practical tools and insights to support women in their entrepreneurial endeavors.

Throughout the highs and lows, I have decoded the tremendous power of resilience, the ability to stand strong in the face of adversity, and the art of reinventing myself when circumstances called for it. I have gathered that failure is not a symbol of defeat but a stepping stone toward personal growth and a driving force for transformation. Each setback I confronted granted me newfound strength, honed my skills, and imparted the wisdom to steer through the dire straits.

So, let us embark on this caravan of self-discovery. Within the depths of my experiences, we will find a renewed sense of purpose, equipped with the required tools and insights to carve our paths. Through our collective learning, we will navigate the uncharted waters of entrepreneurship, always striving to leave a lasting impact and to inspire those who come after us.

This is a tale of resilience, reinvention, and an unflagging pursuit of dreams. Welcome on board.

CHAPTER 1

Finding Myself

"Vision is the art of seeing what is invisible to others."

– Jonathan Swift

"Remember: If the unique ideas were obvious to everyone, there wouldn't be entrepreneurs. The one thing that every entrepreneurial journey has in common is that there are many, many steps on the road to success."

– Tory Burch

Born and raised in the heart of Indore, a small town in Madhya Pradesh, my life began within the warm cuddle of a joint family. The walls of our ancestral home sheltered my parents, uncle, and grandparents, all harmoniously living under a single roof. Ours was a family that emanated humility, simplicity, and single-minded devotion to conservative values. Yet, paradoxically, we held education and learning in the highest regard. It was a unique blend of old-world traditions and modern aspirations, an atmosphere that encouraged growth and understanding.

My mother, a dedicated educationist, was the anchor of our family, managing the complexities of a large household with tremendous finesse. Her ability to balance the diverse personalities and needs within our family was nothing short of remarkable.

In contrast, my father, a sophisticated scholar hailing from Agra University, embodied sophistication and indulgence. His lifestyle was an icon of extravagance, but it was stitched together with threads of discipline. He held a senior position with the prestigious Birla Group, contributing his intellect and expertise to the corporate world. It was an interesting blend, seeing a man who could appreciate the finer things in life while maintaining a regimented lifestyle.

My grandfather, a distinguished courtier serving the king of Neemrana, added an aura of regality to our family's history. His stories of the royal court and his role in the bygone era were a source of endless fascination for all of us.

Although my parents were open-minded, they were exceptionally protective of their daughters, a common trait in a society deeply entrenched in the post-British era. During those times, Indian society clung tightly to rigid belief systems, and the status of women was often perceived as limited, lower, and vulnerable. Male chauvinism and patriarchy were not just accepted; they were respected and glorified norms.

Yet, amidst the backdrop of these oppressive societal norms, as students, my sisters and I were fortunate to lead our lives in an environment of benevolence. We were encouraged to dream, to learn, and to aspire, and that nurturing support from our family became the beacon guiding us through a world that was still struggling to break free from the chains of its history. During my academics, I was an active participant in a myriad of activities. I was not content with merely hitting the books; I wanted to cherish the full spectrum of experiences that college life offered. Sports, cultural events, and college elections were arenas where I eagerly engaged, and my enthusiasm eventually led me to the position of college secretary during my second year of graduation.

My academic performance might have been average, but I compensated with my ability to swiftly grasp complex issues. This knack for comprehension had been my ally since my school days, where I shone in debates, dancing, and sports, earning myself the title of an all-rounder.

Spending five years in a hostel while pursuing my undergraduate degree in Indore and postgraduate studies at BITS Pilani transformed me into a resolute all-rounder. At BITS Pilani, I extended my involvement by joining the music club, relishing song competitions and other cultural activities. Interacting with peers from diverse backgrounds – be it engineering, architecture, or electrical studies – broadened my horizons. It introduced me to a multicultural environment that not only enriched my experiences but also shored up my courage and decision-making abilities.

After completing my postgraduate studies, I returned to my hometown, Nagda, near Ratlam, and embarked on a career as a schoolteacher. My affinity for being around children and sharing knowledge drew me into this profession. However, it did not take long for me to realize that it did not align with my creative aspirations and the rewards were meager. As much as I loved the company of young minds, the repetitive routine of teaching phonics and alphabets left me feeling unfulfilled. It became a monotonous endeavor that stifled my creativity and initiative, and ultimately, my tenure as a teacher was short-lived.

At the tender age of 21, I stepped into the world of arranged marriage, an eventful turning point in my life's book. My husband, an engineer and senior bureaucrat, held devout traditional values, setting the stage for a life that was vastly different from what I had known. The role of a homemaker beckoned, marking a new phase in my life. Raised in a family that favored unconditional respect, acceptance, and belief, I brought with me the enthusiasm and dreams of a young girl.

Marriage is an acute evolution, offering a woman the chance to explore different perspectives within her new family. It requires adaptability, the ability to harmonize and bring happiness to all around. So, I believed and set forth on this new chapter. Moving from the carefree and affectionate sanctuary of my parents' home to accepting a reverse role was an episode laden with challenges. It demanded that I adopt a different lifestyle and assume new responsibilities.

From being the youngest and most beloved in my family, I found myself in a joint family setup, where expectations centered on the only daughter-in-law. Balancing the demands of my in-laws, cultivating a relationship with my husband, and managing the complexities of extended family connections was no small feat. It was a time when I faced personal, emotional, and financial challenges that put my resilience to the test.

Getting married at a young age, I had never aspired to confine myself solely to the role of a homemaker. There was an ever-present yearning within me to explore and nurture my creative abilities. It was a critical part of my being that demanded attention. With this inner crossfire and uncertainty about my future plans, I decided to pursue my B.Ed. from the prestigious Central Institute of Education (CIE) at Delhi University. Teaching, although not my innate passion, granted me a platform to express my creative side. It was around this time that I was blessed with a baby boy, further igniting the flames of my desire to trail something that would provide a deeper sense of creative fulfillment.

In Quest for the Path "Dil hai chota sa.. choti si aasha"

I contemplated the idea of setting forth on a new and challenging venture. The longing for something fresh, something uncharted, had always been the driving force within me. Yet, it seemed like a vast sea of uncertainty, with no clear destination in sight.

At first, I toyed with the idea of starting cooking classes, hoping to share my culinary expertise with others. However, my family members, while dear to me, were not particularly cuisine-conscious, which led me to reconsider. This initial thought swirled away like a wisp of smoke.

Then, another idea began to take shape – perhaps I could establish tuition classes, a child care center, or offer entry courses for students seeking daily guidance in their studies. Yet, these ideas felt all too routine, and the allure of something truly different and innovative eluded me.

My mind was a fertile ground for various ideas, but none took root in the soil of my aspirations. I was new to Delhi, and the vastness of the city, coupled with my limited social circle, made it challenging to discern where to begin. This quest, marked by a gigantic question mark, drove me to explore novel concepts, initiatives, and product lines. I yearned for something that would not only challenge me but also infuse my life with creativity and innovation. It had to be a pursuit that offered not just financial gains but also a deep sense of accomplishment and self-expression.

As my contemplation deepened, I repeatedly asked myself, "What should I start?" It was not a matter of financial necessity, as I was well-provided for. The question that loomed large was how to harness my time more effectively after completing household chores and, in the process, find a way to contribute to the world and my own growth. My upbringing in Indore had been nurturing and peaceful, providing a fertile ground for personal development. However, the transition to Delhi after my marriage was marked by a sharp contrast. The city's hustle and bustle left me feeling like a stranger in a cacophonous crowd. The streets teemed with people, and traffic jams snarled the roads. I was adrift in the sea of the metropolis, unsure of where to anchor my dreams and aspirations.

In my pursuit of something undefined yet compelling, my innate curiosity impelled me to explore. One day, during my leisure time, while browsing through the telephone directory, a particular entry caught my eye – the Business and Professional Women's Association. I dialed the number and arranged a meeting. The association was housed within Lady Irwin College, an institution exclusively for young women.

Upon meeting the members, I discovered a diverse group of individuals representing various professions: college teachers, lawyers, banking professionals, doctors, educationists, and politicians. Excitement and enthusiasm surged within me; I believed I had stumbled upon my dream community, a compass to guide me. But the reality soon unfolded, and I realized that their common goal was to establish a housing society. It was a valuable networking opportunity, but it did not provide the clear direction I sought. It was a lesson learned: do not rely on strangers to solve your personal dilemmas. Once more, I found myself gravitating toward education and teaching as a potential path. In the midst of this indecision, I joined a school to teach English to high-grade students, preparing them for their final exams. I dedicated myself to this role for about eight months, although it coincided with the transformative journey of motherhood as I awaited the arrival of my second child.

In my relentless aspiration for knowledge, one day, I made a decision that led to a new chapter. I enrolled in a five-day training program focused on finance and marketing, with daily sessions lasting two hours. This program was offered by the Small Industries Services Institute (SISI), under the Ministry of Small-Scale Industry. However, like the snakes and ladder game, surmounting obstacles hissed on my path. I hailed from a conservative Marwari family, renowned for their business acumen. Unfortunately, I did not have a background in business.

Despite my husband's support, the majority of my family members were greatly opposed to the idea of a young woman venturing into business. Limited financial resources and a dearth of business knowledge made the journey seem formidable and almost impossible. Doubts and uncertainties settled into my mind like unwelcome guests, contemplating the complexities of handling it all. The decision to start small versus big was another point of contention, further muddling my path with a myriad of "ifs" and "buts."

The Idea of Small Business: First Initiative And First Lesson Or Failure/Success

The feeling of living life bursting with financial freedom and success was so strong and spontaneous that I wanted to try something new and successful. It felt like I always wanted to try something new and flourish in the domain of business.

I was pretty quick as far as getting information on the various subjects was concerned. *I would often be called a 'crazy' person.* I vividly remember my undeviating passion for work, a trait that was quite exceptional among young women in those times. It was a fire within me, a determination to break through the societal norms and expectations that often limited the aspirations of women.

I fondly recollect those days when I would engage my engineer husband in spirited discussions about potential projects and ventures, as we chewed over the idea of establishing a manufacturing unit. We explored a wide array of product possibilities, from twilight switches to solar systems, fly ash bricks to recycled waste, and the imprinting of various products, among other concepts.

Attending bureaucratic and business gatherings, a common practice given my husband's senior government position, provided opportunities to network and seek avenues for our aspirations. I listened intently, my ears and eyes keenly attuned to any faint glimmers of opportunity, but the path remained elusive. The year was 1975, a time when India had yet to experience significant industrial progress and the economy was tightly regulated. We marveled at black and white television sets, and owning a car was a statement of luxury.

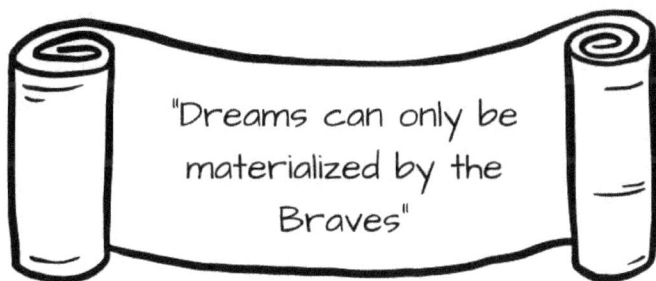

"Dreams can only be materialized by the Braves"

Mobile phones were a futuristic concept, and even having a landline telephone was considered a privilege. Obtaining a landline telephone was no small feat in that era. There was only one formidable provider, MTNL, operating within a bureaucratic labyrinth. The process of applying for and installing a phone line in your home could take up to a year. Undeterred, I, fueled by my determination, visited different offices, met officials, and pleaded my case. However, my efforts seemed in vain.

Then, one day, a helpful officer from MTNL offered a valuable suggestion: apply on medical grounds to expedite the process. Although hesitant and fearful of providing false information, my friend Madhu persuaded me to write the application accordingly. I mentioned in the application that my mother-in-law required urgent medical advice, making a telephone a necessity. Moreover, I argued that a young woman visiting the telephone office, which was a rarity in those days, would draw attention to her grievances and lead to a more favorable response.

That was how the classic rotary dial phone made its way into our home, a small but significant victory. It taught me a valuable lesson: *"If you truly need something, find a way to obtain it, even in the absence of support or a systematic process."*

My inquisitive nature always led me to keep a watchful eye on opportunities and stay updated with the latest developments. In the good old days, it was rather uncommon and, therefore, relatively easy to secure representation for international products in India, as most items were imported. In the 1980s, companies like Pepe Jeans were eager to enter the Indian market. When you sent them letters expressing your interest, their responses were promptly affirmative.

One of my friends, Mrs. Krishna Sahay, who was involved in exporting garments, saw an opportunity to sell Pepe jeans in the Indian market and acquired the agency. Although India was a vast consumer market, the high tariffs and customs duties of the closed economy at the time made it challenging for such products to thrive, rendering the economics unviable. By this time, I had moved away from the hustle and bustle of the joint family setup, living in an independent house with my husband, two small children (aged 2 and 4), and my mother-in-law. After taking care of my family and managing household chores, I found myself with spare time, which I was determined not to waste on passive activities like watching TV or snoozing.

I had a burning desire to engage in something creative. During a social dinner event, my husband and I met a gentleman from Bombay who was in Delhi to appoint an agent to represent his products in Northern India. He owned Polypick Industries, which specialized in Ultra High Molecular High-Density Polyethylene extraction plant products, including sheets, blades for the paper industry, and lining for chemical plants – highly technical items that piqued my interest. To pursue this opportunity, I needed my husband's consent, given his senior position in the government. After some initial hesitation, he granted his approval, thinking it would likely fizzle out in a few months.

Surprisingly, the gentleman readily accepted my offer and terms, providing me with a contract letter. I immediately began searching for a rental space, registered a company, and in 1979, Sears International Private Limited was born. Starting an industrial plastic trading business infused me with new enthusiasm, something different and truly challenging that invigorated my body and mind. My daughter was just two years old, and my son was four. So, I enrolled them in a nearby nursery school and was ready to set forth on my entrepreneurial venture. My single-mindedness edged me forward, and I could not let this opportunity slip through my fingers.

In 1982, I initially started from a small space in my house garage and later secured a small two-room space in Shakti Nagar, New Delhi. One room served as a reception area, and the other was my workspace. I would leave for the office around 9 AM and return by 12.30 PM to be with my children. The pressure to reach home in time always loomed, driven by my determination to be there when my children returned from school, so as not to let my motherly instincts be clouded by guilt.

1982- Industrial Chemicals Laboratory
Created in the Garage at My Home-Instructing my Technical Supervisor

Despite lacking a background in technical products, I would rise early each day and read books on plastics, consulting my husband for explanations on concepts like density and measurement. I had graduated in arts, and my last experience with science had been in the 8th grade. Gaining a deep understanding of these subjects demanded hours of reading, questioning, and writing. Women were not expected to possess knowledge about technical products, but I was committed to starting from scratch, driven by my inquisitive nature and desire to understand everything I encountered. Every day was spent learning about plastics, the molding process, types of machinery, manufacturers, and the uses of different plastics.

During that time, plastic grains were imported under license. This learning process continued for months until I was saddled with enough knowledge and confidence to approach companies about their products. This continued for some time, marking the beginning of my journey into the world of business and plastics.

Thorough Product Knowledge is a Must

"The secret of getting ahead is getting started. The secret of getting started is breaking your complex overwhelming tasks, and starting on the first one."

– Mark Twain

Reflecting on the past, it is truly phenomenal how our generation accomplished things in the absence of modern technological conveniences. No mobile phones, no computers, no internet, and no online systems to access information – we relied on newspapers, articles, and a handful of business magazines for knowledge. Communication and networking happened primarily through associations where you could engage with fellow business people. Creating a company profile was one of the initial steps in introducing my business. I distinctly remember meticulously compiling lists of prospective companies to approach, primarily chemical factories and paper manufacturing companies. Back then, city-wise telephone directories were our go-to source for references, providing complete addresses and landlines, as mobile services were introduced much later in the country.

The process of reaching the right person often involved numerous phone calls and interactions with various intermediaries, requiring substantial effort in coordination, calling, and scheduling appointments. It was indeed a daunting task. Most industries and companies during that era were predominantly managed by men, and characterized by highly hierarchical structures. Breaking through to the right person required relentless persistence. When speaking to potential buyers, they would often assume I was merely an operator – after all, I was a woman. They often insisted on speaking with a male colleague, even when I effectively conveyed information about the product and its pricing. Each time, I had to work hard to convince them that I was the owner and decision-maker. Despite providing ample assurances, there were instances where belief in my authority was hard to come by, forcing me to personally visit or engage in extensive discussions to seal a deal.

This mindset underlined a societal bias that persisted, associating women primarily with domestic roles, regardless of their positions or locations. It was a challenging and responsibility-heavy job. Clients could call me at any time of the day for discussions, and I had to find ways to manage my time effectively while juggling the responsibilities of a mother, wife, daughter-in-law, and my foundational family. The only window that suited me for business was from 9 AM to 12 PM, but I could not share this with anyone, fearing that clients or vendors might perceive me as incapable. I recall an experience with a carpenter who came to repair a table. Upon completing the work, he insisted that I ask my "sahib" (boss) to inspect the piece. I had to assert my authority and clarify that I was, in fact, the boss of the place. This incident underscored that women often needed to be assertive and unmistakably clear to make men acknowledge their authority at all levels, regardless of the differences in roles and positions.

From Peon to CEO- All in One

The first year of business in Industrial plastic was exciting and enigmatic in the sense that the office was more of a 'one-person' show where I worked from the role of an MD to a peon. I had zero ideas about the nuances of business, but had a knack for getting things done. I was happy that I was able to get results in a little time and got the show rolling on the road.

I started visiting several companies with product samples. I was astonished to realize that when I met the owner of the company, his attitude was more respectful than his junior officer. Probably, the owner had respect for a young woman. However, when I met the purchasing officer, there was a strange, inquisitive look in his eyes that made me shirk several times. The attitude was pathetic and irritating at times. I felt devastated. But I had no choice as I had made the choice.

Ultimately, my hard work and persistent approach made a dent, and I had good orders in hand. However, for the customized orders, I was getting exhausted as I had to drive to their office.

Then I had to attend the meeting and get back home before the children came back from their schools. I soon realized that I needed to hire an assistant who could do the follow-up work once the pitching and closing of the deal were almost confirmed. That helped me in expanding my business. After a few months, I employed one more person. The introduction of additional helping hands led me to contemplate expansion and diversification. I started considering the possibility of growing our business and adding more products to our portfolio.

In the very first year, 1982, we achieved a remarkable feat by generating a turnover of about 10 lakh rupees, which, in today's terms, would be equivalent to 1 crore rupees. This was a sizeable sum, especially at that time when many individuals relied on monthly salaries or had modest earnings from their businesses. The success of our initial venture was a tremendous confidence boost, instilling in me the belief that we could expand and diversify our trading business.

To broaden our product offerings, I introduced box strapping tape made of polypropylene. I had the privilege of meeting a gentleman from Mumbai (formerly known as Bombay), who held an engineering degree and was also an alumnus of BITS, Pilani. He introduced me to an innovative packaging concept that immediately resonated with me. I began loading tension machines from Mumbai and box strapping materials into my car, visiting factories in the Faridabad Industrial belt. I would research the names of companies and potential buyers for our products before making my visits. This approach allowed me to connect with several prominent companies and secure their business.

Our product range now included anti-corrosive chemicals, Ultra High Molecular High-Density Polyethylene sheets for anticorrosive lining, polypropylene box strapping, and industrial adhesive chemicals. These products catered to different sets of customers, and the clientele for anti-corrosive chemicals and industrial plastics was relatively limited. Box strapping, on the other hand, opened up a new market segment. Some clients required various products at different times for their distinct needs, making our business more dynamic and versatile.

Finance Requirement

With a growing array of products on our shelves, I found myself in need of additional funds to support the expansion of our trading business. Raising capital was a formidable challenge, particularly in a period when not only was the economy rigid but so were the prevailing mindsets. I pondered over this for a while, as my resources were insufficient to invest further in the business. Filled with a mix of uncertainty and determination, I took the step of borrowing the first loan from the Bank of India with the assistance of a friend who worked at the very same bank. This initial investment was not substantial but provided the necessary support for our trading activities. I also sought help from my father, who agreed to lend his fixed deposits for an overdraft facility to fulfill our financial requirements.

In my hunt for financial sustainability, covering expenses, and achieving profitability, I left no stone unturned. I was fully immersed in the growth of my business, dedicating my time and energy to expanding our current products and exploring new product lines. The marketing aspect of the trading business was relentless. I made numerous calls, introduced products, followed up in writing, and visited prospective clients. Life became incredibly busy and burst at the seams with challenges. After visiting numerous companies and engaging with different individuals, I often felt drained by the end of the day. Juggling my business, kids, and constant search for new products and clients for two years left me exhausted. While the business was growing, and both my family and I had our fair share of triumphs and struggles, I could not help but feel a sense of incompleteness. I could not find answers within myself or from others about what to do next.

My First Failure

To grow, I began adding products from various sources, catering to different customers. I expanded both vertically and laterally, striving to include a wide range of products. The process of acquiring diverse products was as challenging as selling them. Managing multiple salespeople, each handling different products, was quite a demanding task. It felt like a perpetual sprint, as I constantly had to build additional marketing and sales teams, acquire new customers, and establish new sales channels, which required additional capital.

I realized this approach was a misstep, albeit a bit late. Instead of strengthening the existing sales network and developing complementary products, I ventured into unrelated product lines that necessitated entirely new sales channels and teams. This was a pivotal learning experience for me in the world of marketing. While there was unquestionably money and profitability in the trading business, I still felt like I had not quite reached my Eureka moment. After gaining a thorough understanding of the trading business, I believed it was time to transition to manufacturing.

The hesitance I felt was due to a shift in my thought processes, with negative thinking overpowering me to the extent that it was challenging to regain focus on the right thoughts and actions. The realization dawned on me that marketing is indeed the toughest aspect of business and serves as the engine that propels an organization forward. The complex task of managing a bag of primarily unrelated items was quite the undertaking. I share my business experiences because many people have written about how to achieve success and the qualities needed for entrepreneurship. I intend to candidly recount both the failures and successes, presenting a real-life example that encompasses all the ups and downs.

I believe that my upbringing and family background may bear some similarities to yours. Various phases come into everyone's life, and the key is to decide the direction you want to pursue.

I hope this book serves as a mirror that reflects your mindset and skills, potentially accelerating the process of scaling your business to new heights or considering these aspects if you are planning to start an enterprise. If a woman like me, who began with no business acumen from scratch, can achieve this, then so can you!

Challenges

When I go back deep into my memory lane, there was a time when I too was down in the dumps; I had no money in my purse. I had to check my handbag several times before steering my car into the petrol station.

Things were not that easy in the early eighties. Above all, there was no trade or business-friendly atmosphere.

As a woman entrepreneur, you may often find yourself caught in a never-ending rat race. It is a common belief among women that hard work is the sole path to a successful business. However, this is not entirely true. I have experienced the relentless spinning wheel of work that nearly led me to the point of winding up my business. It was during this time that I discovered alternative approaches. Let me continue by sharing some examples and experiences. For women, choosing the right business or career path can be quite challenging. When a woman desires to pursue a profession to meet her financial needs and gain independence, she usually thinks of roles like teaching, working in a bank, becoming a lawyer, or a doctor, depending on her education. The thought of starting a business seldom crosses her mind, and even if it does, she may not know where to begin. Nevertheless, she possesses confidence in her abilities. Overwhelmed by obligations, she craves the freedom of running her own business.

She looks around and observes that some women of her age, or even younger, are running businesses successfully. She sees her friends excelling in jewelry sales or clothing manufacturing. Despite these examples, she remains entrenched in the myth that it is taxing for a woman to become an entrepreneur. She may be hesitant to start on her own, not necessarily out of fear, but because of the reluctance to stumble. Her primary concerns revolve around the multitude of responsibilities at home, primarily her children and then her husband. She admires women who have ventured into non-conventional industries like television manufacturing, paint, electrical appliances, commercial merchandise, chemicals, and agriculture.

However, when she contemplates her own capabilities, doubt and mixed feelings take over. She questions her knowledge and hesitates about taking the risk of arranging finances, managing the business, and successfully organizing marketing efforts. She has no idea where to obtain the necessary capital. She often wonders what will happen if she invests her savings and the business fails. The fear of losing her hard-earned money prevents her from taking the leap, and her startup dreams crumble like a house of cards.

Outcomes and More Learnings

When *you start dreaming* day and night, the obscure path starts getting gradually clear. That is what I learned, which I did not know at that time.

When you aspire to start a business, your first intuition that perpetually subscribes to your mind is that you will win, come high water or tide, and you feel like agreeing to it. With no experience in hand, only your intelligence, commitment, and gut feeling assure positive outcomes. .*"You first need a strong will."*

I am sharing this background with the sincere hope that women who aspire to start something of their own will find the encouragement to do so. It is because every woman experiences these same situations. This wavering thought process is entirely natural, driven by a lack of business experience and self-confidence. Over the last decade, women's entrepreneurship has been recognized broadly as an untapped source of human and economic growth. With the click of a button, awareness, and emphasis on education, Indian women have shifted their interests from the kitchen, handicrafts, and traditional cottage industries to non-traditional, higher activities.

Apart from financial power, a strong desire to capitalize on her own talent has taken up a priority in her life. **As small entrepreneurs, we are supposed to work hard, trek through the hills and valleys and keep forging ahead. This formula of *making headway* applies to the vast majority of us,** as nothing comes easy in life. And business is no exception. There is no secret to success other than motivation and hard work. However, there are times when, despite putting in hard work, you get stuck or the results are at odds. Finally, you are left with failures and frustrations. During such episodes, resilience is the key to success. Like King Bruce, we should try, try and try until we succeed.

But why is it that, especially, women entrepreneurs hit the blind wall more often? Is it because of a lack of support, infrastructure, or finances, or is there some other reason? After a few years, we find that the roller coaster ride is still in full swing. And finally, women may close the business after back-breaking work of 4-5 years.

Remember, an entrepreneur must be like flowing water; making ways to cross through the rocks. Secondly, observe and look for a solution to it.

Ms. Rita Singh, Managing Director, MESCO Steel Company

Mrs. Rita Singh has earned many laurels and brought recognition to the MESCO group. She has won the Federation of Indian Chamber of Commerce and Industry Award for the "Best Woman Entrepreneur of the Decade". She was also the first lady member on the Board of Trade, Govt. of India's highest body for trade and commerce, advising the then Prime Minister, Chairperson of the Council of Leather Exports and Chairperson of FDDI under the Ministry of Commerce. She was the first woman entrepreneur to enter a hard-core male-dominated industry in 1992. The country had just opened up some steel plants for the public. Earlier, it was an undertaking of the Government of India.

Before getting into the export of leather garments, Rita Singh began with a small dairy and Khansari (cottage sugar) unit at Hapur near Delhi. Her meteoric rise was in the early 1990s when the MESCO group forayed into footwear retailing, aviation, shipping, putting up a pig iron plant, and integrated steel complex in Orissa.

According to Mathew Stock, a British Steel Trader and Director of Stemcor, in the Middle East and South Asia, Rita Singh is 'determined' and 'persevering', which are two traits, he says, that are much needed in a highly competitive business like steel. He adds, "Rita also sticks to what she says, an important attribute for a business partner, and is a good commercial head. That (selling out) could not have been the easy option. You have to show a lot of grit and determination to pull through something like this."

How did you start your business? Did you ask for any support for your finances?

I never asked for any money. I sold some of my things, started my first enterprise with Rs. 5000/- and then went to the bank. I wanted to lay the cornerstone of a dairy farm and bought some 200 buffalos and cows on loan. However, I wound up that business after 2 years because the mortality rate of buffaloes and cows is quite high.

Then I went for another business – a small sugar mill.

Did networking help you in your business?

I did a minimum amount of networking for my business. But yes, as I reflect today, I feel I should have done more.

Is it very hard being the only woman in the meeting room? At any stage, did you feel that being a woman is a tough thing stepping into the hard-core industry?

In any business, you are often reminded that you are a woman. But if you do not focus too much on it, that does not make any difference.

How did the mining business idea dawn upon you?

I was in China for my business. Mr. Biju Patnaik heard me talking, he came to me and asked, "Why don't you put up a plant in Orissa?" So we came to Orissa. Mr. Patnaik gave us his full support and thus, we completed setting up the plant in a very short time. At that time, i.e. in the year 1994-1995, the investment was Rs. 350 crores. That was the time when a lot of people got after my life and bombarded allegations.

Yes, there are a lot of issues in the mining business, including politics. But the point is, if you deal reasonably with the employees in this business, things work out because, at the end of the day, they are also human beings.

I was targeted a lot in this business. Many people would pass sarcastic remarks to leave the country. But I replied, "I am not going anywhere; this is my country."

How did you convince bankers, being a woman? Did you feel any hesitation while applying for loans?

No, I never thought that way. I never shrank from putting up my points. I never thought that I did not know anything and doubted my capabilities.

Currently, I am running two steel plants. I have mining plants in Cambodia and Madhya Pradesh.

When you started, were there any angel investors or venture capitalists involved?

No. I did not have any background in business because my paternal family was into education and my husband's family members were *zamindars* (landowners). So, I jumped into the water and did not know how to swim.

I had a small piece of land in my village, so I went to the bank manager and asked if I could get a loan. I did not know how to draft a proposal, so the manager said that he would visit the location and review the possible options. He came to the village and things worked out. After a few months, a loan for the sugar factory was sanctioned.

You are a serial entrepreneur because you have ventured into leather and a lot of other things. What did you do with the sugar factory finally?

In the sugar factory business also, I lost money because the excise was very high and it was the traders who were making profits. Then I realized that small manufacturing did not have that kind of money. I ran that sugar factory business for three years, but whatever loan I had taken was all exhausted.

Normally there are two ways in life – either you give up or you go ahead. So, I decided that I am not going to give up; I am moving ahead. After a prolonged spell of rumination, I found export was the right business for me. I borrowed money from the villagers and took my first step into this business without knowing how I was going to do it.

And why I ventured into so many businesses is because coming from a small business, if you want to become an industry person, then you must have that kind of capital to become an industrialist.

What else do you think you would have done differently?

A lot of things can be done differently. When you start, you do make mistakes. But if you do not err, you will not learn and probably you will not be where you are. I started from a non-business background; I frittered away some of the opportunities that I should have grabbed. For example, I was offered a Rajya Sabha MP seat from BJD by Mr. Biju Patnaik. But I said no because I did not have any political experience. If I had taken that opportunity, I would have had different experiences in my life.

Key Takeaways

- ✤ Dream Big Enough.
- ✤ Follow your dream, talk to your successful entrepreneur friends, and take their advice. Or look for some experienced friends in coaching or trainers. Fix up time with them and discuss the detailed version of your plan with them.
- ✤ Do not invent a new wheel. Learn from what is available.
- ✤ Yearn for creative fulfillment amidst your responsibilities of marriage and motherhood.
- ✤ Engage in conversations with a minimum of three individuals who operate within your field of interest. Inquire about their strategies to expand their businesses. Record your findings and analyze their business growth, financial arrangements, and customer base development approaches.
- ✤ Make notes on these three models with details on product specification, market, finance, investments, customers and process time. This will help you create your approach to your business.
- ✤ If you deeply aspire to become an entrepreneur, enroll in a training program in the same niche.
- ✤ Find some companies in your space and start Googling them, research them thoroughly.
- ✤ Challenges will surely come your way. So, gear up to get comfortable with the uncomfortable.
- ✤ In the initial phase, you may have to play multiple roles, from Managing Director to peon. This endows you with hands-on experience and a learning process in various aspects of the business.

- ✤ You may get the show on the road with one product but keep a close watch on the options to diversify your range of products.
- ✤ Befriend not only successes but also failures, as setbacks are the best teachers. Like flowing water, learn and move on.

CHAPTER 2

Alice in Business Land

"There is no passion to be found playing small - in settling for a life that is less than the one you are capable of living."

– Nelson Mandela

Business Environment

As a business owner, you likely consider numerous dimensions daily, encompassing finance, marketing, inventory, human resources, and many other aspects. However, one crucial factor often overlooked is the ambiance. Ambiance holds great importance in various businesses. It molds your establishment's mood, character, quality, tone, and overall atmosphere.

My initial impression of the United States, during my first visit in 1980, was that it offered a friendly and relatively straightforward process for registering a company. The systems, processes, and overall business culture were not just supportive but also provided a conducive environment for growth and development.

Ambiance can evoke specific feelings and shape how people perceive and engage with your business. Consider whether you would revisit a business based on its environment. The ambiance can influence people's decisions to invest time and money in that particular setting. *"From 1975 to 1985, the business atmosphere in India was not so entrepreneur-friendly compared to other countries like America. The bureaucratic set-up was intense. The inspector raj (rule) was deep-rooted, and entrepreneurs were afraid that any inspector coming to their doorstep meant uncalled problems and was a corrupt, regular money-swindling process.*

In the 1970s, the GDP growth remained more or less at the same level. But in the 1980s, this growth rate catapulted to 5.6 percent; please visit the BSE Sensex and watch it soar during this decade. Ditto with the Index of Industrial Production. Something was happening, though few knew what or how at least initially."- R.N. Bhaskar

"Delhi underwent an unbelievable transformation, thanks to the 1982 Asian Games," **Krishan Datta** wrote in the Business Economy.

"Swept back to power in 1980, she saw the Asian Games as a stage for the government to showcase a shining India to itself and the world. Television was to be the tool. Appu, the tubby elephant mascot of the Games, was also symbolic of the advancing, prosperous nation-state, but taking Appu to the drawing rooms of its citizens required a unified national service, along with an enhanced level of technology to facilitate it. While the expansion of television in the mid-1980s resulted from a confluence of factors, the creation of an indigenous satellite capability, the availability of low-cost transmitters, and the coming together of various policies initiated in the 1970s, it was the Asiad that provided the trigger.

As the host, India had to provide live telecast facilities to other participating countries. When an embarrassed government realised how backward its facilities were, it overhauled unprecedented in the annals of television history. When even Sri Lanka had colour television, it wouldn't look good for India's India to be beaming the Games in black and white, as was the norm until then. So the creation of national service was also accompanied by the introduction of colour television. The overhaul of Indian television and creating a televised national service were to unleash far-reaching changes in Indian society.

Television has been central to the fortunes of Indian advertising, and it expanded exponentially in the 1980s, hand-

in-hand with the setting up of Doordarshan's national television service. Television advertising played a crucial role in the creation of a consumerist ethic and the Indian middle class. Advertising rose by an astonishing 31 times between 198081 and 199091, from Rs 80.8 million to Rs 2,538.5 million. By 1992, India had 34 million television sets, which would not have been possible without the turning point of 1982. The introduction of television was the true legacy of the 1982 Asian Games. The country required capacity creation if India had to look good internationally. The Asian Games, therefore, became the catalyst for sprucing up television and stitching a brand-new suit for it.

The first direct result of the Asian Games was the introduction of colour television and the creation of a national service. Before the Asiad, Doordarshan still operated in black and white, and Vasant Sathe, minister for information and broadcasting, discovered to his horror that even tiny Sri Lanka had colour television."

Nalin Mehta, Today Mirror:

The government was finally forced to set the stage for color & black-and-white Indian TV screens, unleashing a new dynamic into Indian imagery.

Indira Gandhi' was keen to place a TV set in each village so that the entire country could see her face and hear her message. She talked about her dreams for India and how, at that time, there was just one channel—Doordarshan. So when a message went out on television, it was almost inevitable that everyone would watch her face and hear her news. And therein lay the rub.

"With the massive development of the streets of Delhi, new phone lines became available and widened roads to deal with the extra traffic. Doordarshan started colour television broadcasts expressly for the Games. Appu on television.

The Delhi Asiad changed India because it marked the creation of a national television network for the first time. When Indira Gandhi Flashback 1982: The Asian Games that transformed Delhi."

This background was very encouraging. So I plunged into the manufacturing of television sets immediately as the demand for black and white TV was growing exponentially. I had understood that once television penetration started happening in villages and smaller cities, it would catch up and spread like a fire.

'The Purpose for a Bigger Plunge...'

Having achieved a certain level of success and accumulated a sizeable sum of money in my trading business over the past two years, I began to feel the call for something greater. It was a desire to grow on a much larger scale. At the time, the government had plans to introduce television-related components for the Asian Games, and I saw this as an opportunity that I needed to seize. Despite the challenges, I was drawn to the path of manufacturing these components.

The big question that hovered over me was, "How will I do it?" I had no prior knowledge, experience, or background in manufacturing. All I had was a dream, a strong desire for success, a determination to move forward, a will to achieve financial independence, and, perhaps most importantly, a personal need to prove to myself that I could do it.

I began to dream, even though I lacked a solid foundation for this endeavor. Internally, I may have felt a bit uncertain, but outwardly, I projected confidence. I could not share my thoughts with anyone, as this was a journey I had to embark on alone.

Find Your Way Through - Ideation

After much brainstorming and extensive research, in 1982, I decided to sally forth on my project related to TV tuners and televisions. I chose to begin with TV tuners and opted to establish a facility for producing the mechanical components required for them. The initial setup took place in the garage of my home in Hauz Khas. My first step was to learn the fundamentals of a TV tuner, how it operated, the raw materials it required, and its role in ensuring the television's proper functioning. The quality of the tuner was crucial as it directly impacted picture clarity and sound quality, making it a vital component for television performance. TV tuners allow you to receive over-the-air television signals and view them on your TV or computer. To gain a comprehensive understanding of the tuner's intricacies, I visited numerous component manufacturers and explored the component market in Lajpat Rai in Old Delhi.

The suppliers provided valuable insights, and I established collaborations with manufacturers of the mechanical parts. It was quite a journey for a Baniya girl dressed in a saree! Production of the tuners commenced with the support and guidance of an experienced mechanic and supervisor who possessed hands-on knowledge of the product. Around the same time, I also brought in a part-time consultant who could offer expertise on the electromechanical aspects required for creating a quality product. After a few weeks, we outgrew our garage setup and relocated to the Naraina Industrial area. In a matter of months, production became consistent, and we began to achieve impressive numbers.

"Business Planning is critical to success. The creation of a business plan provides insight as to what resources the business needs to reach its goals, determine steps to expand into new markets, and enable forecasting and risks."

'The need for the funds was severe. Without a solid business projection, it was impossible to plan for the present or anticipate future growth prospects. Unfortunately, I had no knowledge about creating such a plan, including profit-and-loss summaries. To address this, I began my search for a reliable chartered accountant.

After consulting with a few individuals, I was fortunate to find a CA who had been referred to me by a friend. With their expertise, we worked on preparing a comprehensive financial plan for my business. This spreadsheet encompassed both current financial status and future projections, outlining the actual financing requirements to kick-start the venture.

To secure the necessary funds, I sought assistance from a friend who helped me approach various banks. Given the circumstances, there were limited options for funding, and the interest rates offered by banks were notably high.

Entrepreneurial Mindset

Developing specific skills and adopting the right mindset are paramount for success as an entrepreneur. Some key skills and attributes that are consequential for entrepreneurs include problem-solving, risk-taking, opportunity spotting, and design thinking. These skills are often required daily in various aspects of running a business, and having an entrepreneurial mindset means cultivating and applying these skills effectively.

Coming up with a new idea is just the beginning; the true challenge lies in building a successful business around that idea. This requires a unique mindset that combines creativity, effective communication, and high motivation to achieve success, while also being open to taking risks and learning from failure.

To thrive as an entrepreneur, one must focus on the "5 Cs": Clarity, Competence, Confidence, Connections, and Communications. These elements help entrepreneurs set clear goals, acquire the necessary knowledge and skills, build self-assurance, establish valuable relationships, and effectively communicate their ideas and vision to others. Effective leadership hinges on **communication**, which not only conveys your intentions but also defines your leadership identity.

The impact of pressure on your communication style is worth considering. How you respond to your team's concerns about their workload when feeling pressured is equally vital. Demonstrating confidence in times of uncertainty is crucial, especially when coupled with empathy. In essence, being a proficient communicator necessitates a mindful approach throughout, striving for concise and straightforward messaging, whether you are engaging with others in person, over the phone, or through email. To excel in communication, mindfulness is paramount.

Imagine yourself as the captain of a ship. Navigating your vessel without knowing how to use a compass can lead to a joyless voyage for both you and your crew. It is not just about having a sense of direction but having absolute **clarity** in your course. In my case, I lacked clarity and vision, merely moving forward without a clear rationale. Eventually, I had to change my entire business line. When introducing change or working toward new objectives with your team, setting clear and attainable goals is paramount. This clarity in leadership is fundamental for making meaningful progress.

Crafting a vision and establishing goals are pivotal aspects of leadership and clarity. The blend of excitement and anticipation with anxiety and trepidation can be challenging, even disorienting, but it is all part of the journey. Once you have achieved success in Communication and Clarity, the natural progression is Connection. Building stronger relationships with your team starts with introspection. It is the ability to be grounded and nurture stability in both our emotional and physical domains, bridging the gap between ourselves and others. Forming connections with others is an inherently vulnerable act, and while it may be daunting, the benefits far outweigh the risks. To make substantial progress, you must set deadlines for these goals. Break down tasks into manageable segments, prioritize them, and organize your schedule accordingly.

In every journey, there are, at the very least, two paths to choose from: moving forward into the unknown, toward new possibilities, or retreating and stagnating, doing what we have always done, sticking to the familiar, and reaping the same results.

Confidence is a powerful tool that propels us to new horizons, promotes fresh relationships and yields new outcomes. Having confidence in your abilities, choices, and overall business health allows an entrepreneur to remain composed even during challenging times. This optimism remains essential for long-term success, even in the face of crises. I had strong inner confidence but was equally driven by emotions. Emotions can have a limited yet distinctive role; they can sometimes hinder rather than help.

Thus, maintaining emotional balance is central to practical decision-making and safeguarding your confidence.

Leadership **competencies** include social intelligence, conflict resolution, and interpersonal abilities. They also encompass learning agility, effective decision-making, and the art of building and leading a cohesive team. This forms a vital and integral part of leadership. Being recognized as an industry expert is associated with the capacity to adapt to changing circumstances, fostering a positive work environment, setting clear expectations, and offering continuous support and feedback. To achieve this, self-awareness is a key asset.

Growth and Challenges

Within two years, that is, by 1984, our production had increased; doubled, and tripled, and we were competing with established manufacturers of both TV tuners and their components. At that time, there was one big name in tuners; Chawla Tuners, whom we had to compete with. So, I focused on quality and robust marketing.

All the eminent and large companies were on our clients' list. We had orders from Continental Devices India Ltd., Uptron Ltd. (all five units), Bush India Ltd., Videocon Pvt. Ltd., and so on and so forth.

In 3-4 months, there was exponential growth, the manufacturing figure of 100 tuners per day had gone to 1000 tuners per day. The process of elimination and correction was quick and fast. We had almost 20 people on our payroll, and 40-60 workers on a contract basis. It was easier to hire a worker on a contract basis.

Even though the work was in full swing to the best of its capacity, all was not easy. Several issues started cropping up, that required acumen and management.

Now, despite the quality assembly of the tuner, the mechanical portion would always be in shortage, and I started facing competitors' wrath. They started poaching my skilled workers. It was something I was not prepared for.

We got to grips with another acute issue when our long-term mechanical parts supplier, Bhushan Components, suddenly restricted our supply. We had been heavily reliant on them for our mechanical components. This abrupt change was triggered by the growing demands from emerging TV tuner manufacturers who were offering cash payments to our supplier, in contrast to our credit-based dealings. This enticed our supplier to expand their client base, overlooking our prior arrangements and relationship.

As a result, our production suffered due to a shortage of essential raw materials needed to meet our targets. The situation was complicated because our operations were intricately interconnected, spanning from marketing to the production of finished products and the procurement of raw materials. I was deeply concerned and made efforts to bridge the supply gap by exploring new suppliers who would accept reduced credit terms. Unfortunately, these attempts were met with challenges, either in terms of quality issues or an inability to meet our demands.

At this point, we recognized the need to explore alternatives, such as finding a new supplier capable of providing high-quality mechanical kits. Alternatively, it led me to ponder whether the internal production of these kits could be a viable solution. This way, we would not only fulfill our internal demands but also potentially serve other small-scale tuner manufacturers. The question arises: Is vertical integration the answer to our supply chain woes?

Innovation And Spreading Your Risk- Blending Innovation Is The Solution To Your Problems

In response to the growing demand for tuners and the need for a stable supply chain, we made the strategic decision to expand our production by opening a factory in Noida. After securing a plot in the industrial zone, we began preparations, and by 1985, we initiated manufacturing operations. The facility was substantial, with construction reaching up to the first floor, spanning a vast area of 600 yards. This represented a giant leap in scale compared to our initial micro-unit in Naraina village.

Recognizing the ever-increasing demand for tuners, I also decided to plunge into in-house production of hardware components. My husband played a pivotal role as a staunch supporter in this endeavor. We set up the necessary infrastructure to manufacture the mechanical parts, and as a result, we quickly scaled up our production capacity for tuners, attracting large orders. With ample space and spare capacity, we were poised to meet the surging demand and expand our presence in the market.

Bollywood Replayed Live in My Office –

The Indian labor system rules: Labor Unions, strikes, demands and a 'woman'

The unexpected strike by 80 percent of my factory workers was a shocking turn of events, something I had only seen in Bollywood movies but never imagined it would happen. I felt overwhelmed and shaken, struggling to cope with the situation. Despite the initial shock and anxiety, I decided to confront this challenge head-on.

We sought the assistance of a labor consultant to address the situation. However, I was disappointed when the consultant recommended meeting the workers' demands. My perspective, on the other hand, was focused on achieving a complete victory. I believed that giving in to the workers' demands at that moment would set a precedent and encourage them to repeatedly raise their voices and make demands, assuming they would be met.

The workers' demands included a two-fold salary increase and additional conveyance allowances. My approach was to link salary hikes with target accomplishment. I proposed that if they achieved specific production targets, their salaries would be raised, and incentives would be provided. This approach was aimed at promoting a results-oriented work culture and discouraging a pattern of frequent demands without a corresponding increase in productivity. The workers went on strike with the CITU

Trade Union. They continued to demand that salaries should be increased. The unfaithful and crock were becoming a part of them.

I neither had that kind of money to meet their demands nor the intention. But even if we had the money, probably I would have taken the same decision. Knowing very well that the owner of this factory was a woman, the CITU leader landed in the office in my absence and entered my chamber by pushing his way through. I had no idea about it at all. When I reached my office, I was horrified. I found a man sitting right in front of my desk. In my room, 4-6 workers were standing around him. As soon as I entered and went to my seat, this stranger continued to occupy the chair.

An unauthorized person reclining on my chair brazenly, in my room was completely unacceptable. I was outraged in my mind. I did not know who he was and as if I did not want to know. I immediately asked him to get up from the chair. My factory workers came forward to introduce him to me. After my point-blank remarks, he looked through me and made me feel creepy and uneasy. A few moments passed. I was feeling outrageous and in agony. My boys then reiterated that he was one of the leaders of the CITU Union of Okhla. At that moment, nothing mattered, I did not care. I was in pain and anger at the same time. Again, my instant reaction was to ask him to get up from the chair.

In response to that person's criticism, I listened patiently, but I could not help but feel annoyed by his demeanor. He came across as overweight and impolite, which added to my irritation. I replied to him with a sense of determination, "Listen, sir, these young workers who are part of our team are hardworking and innocent. People like you often attempt to manipulate them into making wrong choices. You encourage them to give you a portion of their wages, enjoy lavish meals at their expense, and live a luxurious life.

You share drinks and snacks with these vulnerable individuals, all the while leading them to believe that you will take care of them. After months of manipulation, you present them with dreams that are neither achievable nor realistic. Whether they can provide for their families becomes inconsequential to you. Your only goal is to manipulate and exploit them for your gain, so you can continue to indulge in fine dining. People like you take advantage of vulnerable people, and your intentions are far from genuine."

After expressing my frustration and venting out some blunt words, I faced the workers in a state of torment and anguish. I told them that those who wished to leave with the individual who had confronted me could do so, and those who wanted to continue working could return by the 13th of that month. Remarkably, 80% of the workers chose to come back and resume their work, demonstrating their commitment to our company. The remaining 20% did not return the next day. However, within the following month, only two workers remained with the union, and the majority of them rejoined our workforce. Some workers opted to pursue opportunities with other companies, but many of them remained loyal and continued working with me.

This decision immensely bolstered my confidence and strengthened my connection and humility with the workers. Despite being a woman, I was not afraid to make a bold decision. I had a strong conviction that yielding to their threats would only encourage them to repeat such actions and perceive me as weak. ***Focus on your gut feeling.***

Financial Management and Bureaucratic Bottlenecks in India

Securing the necessary funds was a critical step for our operations, and I decided to obtain a loan for machinery from the U.P Financial Corporation, as well as working capital from Canara Bank, to ensure a smooth start. This was a consequential move to facilitate our business's growth. However, the process of obtaining these loans was far from straightforward.

It involved numerous follow-ups and meticulous adherence to all the required formalities. After a prolonged and challenging pursuit that demanded an immense amount of time and effort, as well as a fair share of tears and unwavering determination, all the loans were finally sanctioned. With the funds in hand, we were able to install the necessary machinery, marking a prominent milestone in our quest. Also, at that time, the Government of Uttar Pradesh was offering subsidies for establishing industry in Noida, for which I decided to submit my documents and plan.

I vividly recall the experience at the UP Financial Corporation office in Noida, where a lady was in charge. I must apologize for my choice of words, but it seemed like she was determined to make the formalities as challenging as possible for me. Her actions felt like a form of harassment, causing me immense frustration and stress.

Every time I visited the office, she would come up with excuses or pretexts to delay and complicate the process. It felt like a deliberate effort to create obstacles. I could not help but feel betrayed and irritated, however, I had no choice but to endure this with a grain of patience. It appeared that she expected certain favors from me, perhaps hoping for financial assistance. She mentioned that her brother had purchased a piece of land and implied that I should make the payment for that purchase. Unfortunately, I did not have the funds to accommodate such requests.

Have you heard the story of the snakes in a jar without a lid? The two Indian snakes pull the other co-mate and they are unable to escape the jar, whereas the Japanese and American snakes slither away in no time. So is India, and in my experience, at times women themselves can play that limiting role to ensure that others do not succeed.

So, a great deal of delay took place. We followed it up for 12 long years, but all our efforts landed in a bin. They would promise something and would say at the end that they did not have money. I think myriad entrepreneurs did not get subsidies from the UP Govt. for setting up the industry in Noida. This was a classical corruption grip the economy was trapped in.

Operations and Management

After working out all the details of mechanical, plastic, and electronic plants, we got all the dies made, which took almost two to three months. We purchased all the machines, including the lathe machine, hand press, cutting machine, and die casting; and for plastic components as well. I hired a supervisor under whose instruction the work started, including machinery purchase.

As we continued to operate, we found that our machinery's full capacity was not being utilized for the production of tuners, resulting in idle capacity. In response, we made the strategic decision to explore additional opportunities by participating in railway tenders for machined products. This marked the beginning of our lateral expansion and cross-channel distribution efforts.

To facilitate this expansion, we opted to register with the SISI (Small Industries Services Institute). At the time, this registration was essential for obtaining price benefits as a small-scale industry, and it also meant that the tender security money required was largely reduced for registered businesses.

We successfully secured a tender from the Railways, and it involved fierce price competition. Our task was to manufacture buffer assemblies for the railways. We would source die-cast buffer assemblies from Baroda, Gujarat, and then perform the necessary machining at our factory using large lathe machines. As we continued to work on various tenders over a few months, I realized that the entire system, from procurement to receiving payment, involved allocating a certain percentage of funds to various departments and stakeholders. This experience underlines the complexity of working within the tender and procurement processes.

I always felt and experienced that small-scale companies already had so many constraints. Generally, there was a lack of good human resources, especially at the managerial level. All the small and big decisions had to be taken by you only, and there was nobody to guide you. In my opinion, generally, women have a strong gut feeling, which is their big guiding force. Whenever I followed my gut feeling, I made the correct decisions.

"Listen to your sixth sense. Whenever I felt totally stuck, I relied on my gut as the guiding light." During the initial setup in Naraina, when the production increased, the supervisors and other workers tried to get things in their hands by instigating other workers to achieve the production targets. It became apparent to me that the workers were motivated by a desire to maintain their sense of importance, which often led to the formation of worker groups and attempts to exert control. I grasped this psychology quite well, and in response, I adopted a management approach that combined both a friendly demeanor and a firm hand. Nevertheless, managing these dynamics was a challenging task.

The Beginning of a New Journey: Yet Another Leap

It was yet another leap of faith when I decided to plunge all the way and manufacture televisions.

Gender Predisposition, Mindset, Bias Against Women:

The adventure to start manufacturing TV sets was met with unexpected challenges. When I applied for the license to manufacture televisions with the district industries office, the initial response was disheartening. A month and a half later, I was informed that my project had been rejected while others had been granted the license. This news left me perturbed and uneasy, as I could not figure out what was lacking in my project.

Upon meeting with the concerned officer to seek clarity, I was met with a discouraging response. The officer stated, "Madam, it is not a kitty or a social get-together to run a TV industry. It's not possible to handle such a large project by women." This statement was grounded in a biased attitude that presumed that women's participation in business organizations and government advocacy platforms was primarily for social gatherings and parties.

In the face of such discrimination and gender bias, I remained resolute in my determination to overcome this obstacle. Although my heart was heavy, I held onto a single mission. After engaging in numerous arguments and discussions, the proposal was reconsidered by the selection committee. Finally, with tears in my eyes, I received the approval for my black-and-white television project. The decision to set up a television manufacturing unit marked a considerable and bold step. The contrast between the cost of the tuner, which was around 75-80 Rs. per unit, and the cost of the TV set, which ranged from Rs. 3500 to £4000 per unit, was substantial. Establishing a television manufacturing unit required a substantial capital base and a much larger operational space.

At this point, my husband made the courageous decision to join me in this venture, resigning from his secure and respected bureaucratic position. As for me, I recognized the need for a shift in mindset to transition into the world of manufacturing. I understood that I had to acquire new skills and raise the necessary capital to make this venture a success.

I also realized the weightiness of seeking advice from experts who could help me overcome my fears and develop from a creative individual into a capable CEO capable of running a profitable business. My goal was not just limited to personal success but also to contribute to the community and give back to society. I was determined to transform myself into someone with a higher purpose in life, committed to making a positive impact on a broader scale. The seeker and learner in me were never weary of any degree of challenge, instead beaming with energy and newness. I joined the Small Industries Service Institute (SISI) program under the Ministry of SSI, which used to conduct finance, marketing, and management classes.

So, in addition to the work-in-progress, I enrolled in their programs for finance and marketing. This course helped me understand the nitty-gritty of finance, which otherwise looked like a Gordian knot to me. On the program's valedictory day, the Institute invited the chief guest Dr. Chakradhari Aggarwal, Head of the National Alliance of Young Entrepreneurs (NAYE). I was earnestly looking for a platform to connect with some entrepreneurs in Delhi where I could learn something more. I saw an opportunity in this and I immediately joined it. This platform helped me establish contact with government departments and understand business nuances. It also bolstered my overall understanding in many more ways. For the first time, I realized that one needs a platform to meet new people and interact with them successfully.

Despite my membership in the National Alliance of Young Entrepreneurs, the outcome did not align with my initial expectations. The presence of an all-male membership created a reluctance to openly address my challenges and seek their guidance, although the exact reasons for this hesitancy were unclear at the time. Furthermore, due to my status as a small-scale entrepreneur, I lacked the financial means to hire a consultant. Despite all the media buzzing around entrepreneurship, the American women entrepreneurs most people can name were Oprah Winfrey and Martha Helen Stewart.

Then there was another from the UK, Anita Roddick, the Body Shop founder. In India, Simone Tata brought Lakme into cosmetics. And I found the entrepreneurs coming up with me were Rita Singh, MD of MESCO Steels, and Shahnaz Hussain, founder of the Shahnaz Husain Group. We all were first-generation entrepreneurs. Then there were entrepreneurs like Kiran Mazumdar of Biocon or Simon Tata of Lakme who had a strong backup of their father or husband. In fact, the first-generation entrepreneurs were quite exceptional as they went against the tide and established themselves.

None of us were trained businesswomen, but we all had one ingredient in common; *restlessness and a strong desire to achieve. It was this entrepreneurial spirit that drove us.* We also recognized our strength to walk our path.

The Myth of Overnight Success

The inflating consumer demand for televisions was a substantial assurance of the market, but I never thought that I would get stuck due to the fault of others. Big industries were not making timely payments, and the dealers from other estates were manipulating procurement and costs. At that stage, finance became a crucial and challenging issue, more than anything else. I was beginning to question myself and beginning to self-doubt. I wondered if I did not know how to handle it; maybe it was not my cup of tea and I tried to be overconfident in my abilities to manage things. I did not know what to do. Should I take an exit from the business if the production and targets are not met by the deadline? What if I am not able to deliver the goods timely? I used to feel perturbed. Internal crossfire would continue in my mind.

One day, as I sat in quiet contemplation, I delved deep into introspection. Suddenly, a profound realization emerged in my mind. It struck me that God had created a list, and I found myself at the top of it. I interpreted this as a divine sign that I had been entrusted with the responsibility of caring for the hundreds of families working under my management and within my company. I pondered whether I possessed the capability to shoulder their burdens and responsibilities.

I further contemplated what would happen if my name were removed from the top of that list and replaced with someone else's. Would that bring me contentment and peace? This moment of reflection was instrumental in curing my negative thoughts. I resolved that I had to move forward with determination, ensuring that everything fell into its rightful place.

I am sure you have experienced a strong desire to achieve something, yet there is a lingering hesitation that holds you back. After deep and prolonged reflection, I uncovered why women, including myself, sometimes feel out of place or uneasy when handling critical matters, particularly within our businesses.

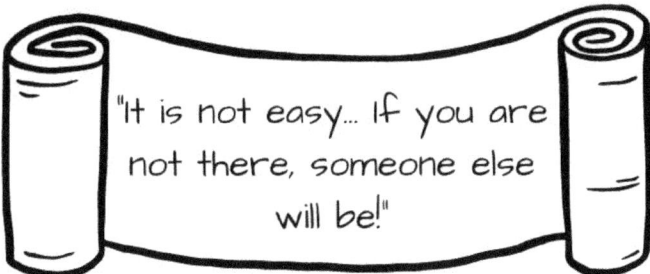

"It is not easy... If you are not there, someone else will be!"

Identify Your Limiting Beliefs

I too felt so and came to the following conclusions:

1. I am afraid, maybe I do not know what I should know, so I will not be taken seriously.
2. People dealing with me will analyze my skills, education and age more closely than that of men.
3. Though I know, I am not sure of what I think is acceptable or not.
4. I will have to spend more time on business, and my children and husband will feel bad about it.
5. I have no business background. Will I be able to do it or not?
6. I am not good at finance.

So on and so forth. It continues from time to time at different stages. The negatives of the brain act like Velcro, and the positives of the brain act like Teflon.

This phenomenon occurs irrespective of one's geographic location. Societies worldwide tend to prescribe certain norms for the behavior of boys and girls. In India, for instance, even in the first-grade textbook, there are instructive sentences: "What is your mother doing?" with the expected response being "Mom is cooking food in the kitchen." Similarly, "What is your father doing?" is met with the response "Papa has gone to the office."

These dialogues leave a lasting imprint on the minds of both girls and boys from their early childhood. Girls are conditioned to believe that their primary role is to prepare meals at home, while fathers are expected to be the breadwinners. Boys, too, grow up with a similar understanding. These deeply ingrained social gender norms are notoriously resistant to change.

Additionally, girls are often subjected to specific behavioral expectations, including being polite and demure, whereas no equivalent standards apply to boys. Consequently, as children, we begin to harbor self-doubts, questioning our abilities and appearances with statements like "I am not good at this" or "I am too skinny." These self-criticisms can solidify into a pervasive belief that "I am not enough." They transform into a persistent inner voice that repeatedly tells us we fall short.

The question then becomes, how can we address this complex issue?

3 Internal Fears That Could Stop Me From Becoming A Business Owner:

1. Can I be a good businesswoman? I suspect that I may not assimilate issues appropriately or have the appropriate thought process to talk to the staff as a leader.
2. I do not have enough experience to handle money and finance.
3. As a businesswoman, I believe one should have umpteen psychological, spiritual, and mental abilities to handle **critical** situations. I doubted I had.

These were some fears I had in my mind before taking off as a business owner. And I am sure, most women encounter most or all of these.

3 External Fears:

1. I have never taken any formal training.
2. People will laugh at me if I fail.
3. Will anybody support me in this activity?

I realized that I was missing several qualities central to being an entrepreneur, which I divided into the following steps.

Lesson learned:

Replace "I am busy' with "I am easy, I am light."

Replace "I do not have time" with "I have enough time for myself, for my family, for my work, and for my sleep."

Replace "I am tired" with "I am fresh, I am perfect, I am energetic."

Ms. Shahnaz Husain,
Founder, Chairperson and Managing Director,
Shahnaz Group of Companies, New Delhi

"She has dominated the market from the USA to Asia. During the 1990s, the average growth rate of her company, which is based in New Delhi, was nearly 19.4%. In the year 2002, her company touched $100 million. Her works are really praiseworthy and have been appreciated all over the world. She has received many awards, such as "The Arch of Europe Gold Star for Quality", "The 2000 Millennium Medal of Honor", *Shahnaz Husain is a name to reckon with. To her exclusively goes the credit of bringing the therapeutic values of herbs out of the mists of antiquity and legend, and combining them with scientific research and practice. Shahnaz Husain has done so much for India's image abroad that she truly deserves the sobriquet of India's Beauty Ambassador.*"

– Washington Post

Was being a woman a hindrance in any way?

Being a woman was not a deterrent for me, as I started a business that dealt mainly with women. I believe that it is a woman who can truly understand the beauty needs of other women. I opened my first herbal salon in my own home so that I could be at home to take care of the needs of my children and family. I was at home when my children came back from school. This way, I was privileged to be endowed with the support and understanding of my family. My salon also provided employment for women. I trained them in beauty, my specialized treatments, and customized beauty care.

Did networking play a role in expanding your business nationally and internationally?

Yes, networking did play a major role in magnifying my business. However, today the word networking implies social networking, but I acclimatized this adage to business networking. Five decades ago, when I launched my first herbal salon, there was no social networking or online business. Very early in my career, I began to encourage ordinary homemakers to open salons in their own homes, so that they could gain financial independence and yet be close at hand to attend to their homes and family. I trained them and offered the Shahnaz Herbal franchise. This was the beginning of my unique franchising system, as well as my beauty training academy. I did not invest in the franchise salon and had no part in the profit or loss of the franchisee's business. But the franchise salons became outlets for my treatments and products. The franchisee could earn a margin of profit on the sale of products. This system of networking is the key player behind the fast-paced extension of my franchise salons. It helped to popularize my specialized salon treatments and my therapeutic products. It also bolstered me to establish the Shahnaz Herbal and Shahnaz Husain brand. Apart from strong branding, the franchisee buttresses my research and development, as well as the innovation of products for which we are known.

Would you like to share some anecdotes/specific examples of how networking helped you?

Even at a time when the demand for the product is sustained through advertising, I did not rely on commercial advertisements. Instead, I banked on "word of mouth" and the fact that a satisfied client is the best advertisement. It was a unique method of establishing goodwill and the importance of customer experience. I also adopted a unique method by attending the inauguration of franchise salons, providing free consultations, and holding a press conference. Thus, the new salons received phenomenal media coverage. Soon, I was flying all over the country, to every city and town, inaugurating franchise salons, addressing press conferences, and speaking to people. It was all based on personal interaction, where I met people, listened to their problems, and provided solutions. Thus, I was answering a human need. Within the first year, 80 franchise salons opened in India. The strategy proved so successful that later I adopted it for the openings of franchise clinics and other ventures abroad. The word was spreading and, unknowingly, a brand was born.

What mantra would you like to share with us? You have been very successful in the international market.

It is true that my success in the international arena, in the face of great odds, is truly magnificent. When I entered the international market, I fought a lone battle, competing with the biggest brand names in a market, where billions of dollars are spent on advertising and packaging. But I projected my solo "India and Ayurveda" image. I also allowed my products to speak for themselves. The fact that I adopted a holistic system like Ayurveda is also the driving force behind my success. I increased awareness of the chemical ingredients in cosmetics and spoke on Ayurveda at beauty congresses and press conferences. You may start small, but think "big". Think that nothing is beyond you. And never give up. I believe one should never stop trying. If you keep forging ahead, you cannot fail.

How did you manage marketing? Please suggest some tips on how women should market their products and scale up their businesses.

Yes, of course, we employ professionals for marketing and sales. We have a dedicated Marketing Department and also an Exports Department to market our products in the international market. I was invited by Harvard Business School to speak on how I created an international brand without commercial advertising. Subsequently, I became a Case Study for Brand Creation today. I am a subject at Harvard for "Emerging Markets" and a part of their curriculum. The secret of success in entrepreneurship and the business world lies in marketing strategies. My marketing methodologies are an unprecedented example of successful marketing with a difference. To women who want to be entrepreneurs, I would say that professional qualifications and training are the order of the day. So, it is essential to acquire professional and vocational training in the field. If you can pursue advanced training and also specialize in some aspects, it can be an advantage. Have the ability to adapt, because one has to blend according to the changing demands of the market and trends. Innovation and creativity are important for success in entrepreneurship.

What have you done differently to achieve your goals?

The unique features of our marketing and business strategies have made my organization stand apart from the rest. I followed the "Word of Mouth" marketing, instead of commercial advertisements. As already mentioned, I believe that a satisfied client is the best advertisement. I followed customized beauty care, with a personal touch and based on individual needs. My products grew out of our clinical treatments. Also, I established an integrated system of Salon Treatments and Product Excellence, which rely on each other. We also adopted the franchise system for extending our treatments, salons, retail outlets, and other ventures. This way, we have fabricated a global network of Shahnaz Herbal franchise ventures.

What is the area where you felt shaken or doubtful about your business acumen?

While training in London, I was horrified by the damage caused by chemical ingredients and treatments. I started wondering if I had taken up the right field. That was when I decided to find an alternative that was safe and without risks. It was my family's faith in herbal remedies and my study of Ayurveda that convinced me that nature and natural means could provide the answers to beauty care. So, I adopted a new concept of natural care and cure and opened my first herbal salon in my home. That was not just a major turning point but also gave an entire direction to my career and future. Obstacles and hurdles come up in life, but I have tried to meet them as challenges, with my desire to excel, my relentless determination to succeed, an iron will, and sheer hard work. I believe that nothing is impossible. You can be what you will yourself to be. You can ink your own destiny.

Key Takeaways

- ☙ Be mindful of the "5 Cs" - Clarity, Competence, Confidence, Connections, and Communication.
- ☙ You may bump into challenges, such as the shortage of raw materials and the unexpected strike by workers. In such scenarios, focus on adaptability and innovative thinking.
- ☙ Your intuition plays a prime role during the bumpy ride. Confront hardships with determination and conviction.
- ☙ Your introspection on limiting beliefs, both internal and external, provides valuable insights. To prevail over these, you can enroll in programs and seek advice, or take a proactive approach to personal and professional development.
- ☙ Do not let yourself get carried away by the myth of overnight success. Remember, there is no shortcut.
- ☙ Engage with industry associations and networks to stay informed about government schemes and subsidies.
- ☙ Leverage digital platforms and official government portals for transparent communication and application processes.
- ☙ Diversify funding sources; explore options beyond traditional banks, such as private lenders or venture capital.
- ☙ Build strong relationships with financial institutions and keep detailed records to streamline future transactions.

- ✎ If required, seek support from higher authorities within the financial institution or escalate the matter to regulatory bodies.
- ✎ Conduct regular operational audits to identify underutilized resources.
- ✎ Explore diversification or partnerships to maximize machinery usage.
- ✎ Implement transparent communication channels to address worker concerns.
- ✎ Build a strong network within the industry for insights and guidance.
- ✎ Invest in technology for streamlined procurement processes.
- ✎ Invest in continuous learning and skill development programs.
- ✎ Collaborate with institutions that promote women in business.
- ✎ Diversify the client base to mitigate risks associated with delayed payments.
- ✎ Establish clear financial policies and terms with clients.
- ✎ Regularly practice positive affirmations and mindfulness.
- ✎ Celebrate small victories and acknowledge personal and professional growth.

CHAPTER 3

Gearing for Success

"Life is like riding a bicycle. To keep your balance, you must keep moving."

– Albert Einstein

"The only limit to our realization of tomorrow is our doubts of today."

– Franklin D. Roosevelt

Scaling Up

We proudly launched our own black and white television under the name "Sonnet," initially introducing it as a 14-inch TV. This marked an eventful moment in our venture. To promote and market our product, we utilized radio ad jingles, as it was the primary media channel of the time. At that point, Doordarshan was the sole TV channel in India.

Our target market extended to the hilly states across the country, including Himachal Pradesh, Uttarakhand, J&K, and other regions. The electronic assembly of tuners, apart from Noida, was initially conducted in Naraina, located in the northwest of Delhi. As our operations expanded, we decided to relocate the electronic assembly to Okhla, which was closer to my residence in South Delhi.

We were relentless in our efforts to penetrate the market, supported by a robust manufacturing process. We prioritized supply chain integration to ensure the highest quality of our products and never compromised on producing the very best. This dedication led to the creation of a competitive advantage, and we experienced significant growth with renowned television manufacturers beginning to source components from us.

We managed to secure the account of "Nicky Tasha", the TV brand of the Escorts Group, to supply television sets as well as TV tuners. All the suppliers providing complete sets of TVs to this company started buying the tuner components from us.

It was a big breakthrough to become a supplier to this 1000 Crore company, back in the 1980s.

Nicky Tasha had captured a gigantic market for black-and-white television in India and we were their biggest suppliers. They had strict quality standards, and we delivered high-quality components.

I always believed in offering value not only in terms of technical products but also in products that offer high performance and standardization.

Nicky Tasha's inspection team used to come and inspect the goods as per their circuitry details, and they were doing random checking of product performance. They used to sign at the back of each product that was tested and checked. So, our head of the production team took care of all the aspects when Nicky Tasha's team visited the factory.

The second big account we secured was 'UPTRON' television, owned by the state government in Lucknow, Uttar Pradesh. Uptron India Limited (later renamed Uptron Powertronics Limited) was a public sector electronics company known for its black-and-white televisions in the 1980s and was primarily involved in trading. They had five television units, all of which were our customers.

Between 1984 and 1986, I became deeply engaged in organizing events for women entrepreneurs within the NAYE association and assumed the role of Vice President.

1984 - Representing Women in Business at the President's House, With Former President of India, Giani Zail Singh

Whenever we planned an event or workshop focussed on women entrepreneurs, I actively sought sponsorships from various SMEs and successfully raised substantial funds from the Naraina Industrial Area. This experience played a key role in boosting my self-confidence and honing my business skills.

With my increasing involvement in the association, in 1989, I received momentous recognition. I was chosen as an Asian Woman Entrepreneur by the Government of Finland to participate in a six-week program focused on export marketing through Prodec. This program was conducted in collaboration with the Helsinki School of Economics, Finland, as part of its Development Cooperation efforts.

In 1988, I received the prestigious *National Award for "Outstanding Entrepreneur" from the Government of India*. This was a dream I had cherished for a long time.

*1988 - 'Outstanding Entrepreneur of the Year' Award
from Former President of India, Mr. Ramaswamy Venkatraman*

Receiving an award from the Government of India was not just an achievement; it was my life's passion and aspiration.

The moment of receiving this award from the President of India at the Vigyan Bhawan ceremony was the most precious and proud moment for me and my family. It marked a tremendous sense of accomplishment and recognition of my dedication and hard work as an entrepreneur.

Challenges

Delivering excellence in quality was a major concern in Tuner production as well as Television production. In an endeavor to ensure that the quality production manager delivers zero-defect tuners, I undertook training for one month in ERTL, Okhla, and learned the technical skill of soldering, and the ways to fit a good quality solder. We faced issues such as alignment of parts which was a big problem.

We were facing problems like the transistors and the capacitors would fall off or would be loose if the worker was not quality conscious. As there was no automation, workers used to do all the work by hand. That training gave me much insight into handling and discussing the product with the production manager or quality expert.

Besides acquiring business skills, I soon realized that learning technical know-how and product knowledge was of utmost importance to be on the top of the game. I had to learn the ropes myself and this way; I was able to intermittently check the micro-production quality efficiently with a quality supervisor and manage issues smoothly.

Market Trends and Competition

Managing the production of television sets was a complex endeavor, given that there were over 352 components to be developed for the production line. To ensure the smooth operation of the supply chain, it was imperative to consistently maintain and keep track of all 352 components. Even a shortage of just one item in the stock could halt the entire production line. Considering that the cost of one TV set was approximately Rs. 3500/-, a shortage of one component could result in severe financial losses, amounting to hundreds of thousands.

Administering and maintaining the inventory of all these electromechanical components was an enormous task, and it demanded rigorous quality inspection and continuous quality maintenance. To simplify the process, I decided to separate the electronics and hardware components. This division made it somewhat more manageable, and maintenance and control became easier.

Assigning Team captains for each account and scaling up. As our business was expanding, and we were supplying televisions to various brands, I recognized the need for additional expertise to scale up our operations. I decided to bring in a consultant to oversee our operations on the factory floor and help identify and source different integrated circuits for various companies. Scaling up our production required the development of distinct teams of workers for different companies, and we allocated tasks accordingly to ensure efficiency and meet the demands of our diverse clientele.

An Ordeal with a Big Industrial House

It may be hard to believe, but this is a true story. The electronics industry is driven by rapidly evolving technology. One of our major clients, a prominent industrial conglomerate, had developed a specific protocol for their TV, altering the circuits. However, they were unable to succeed due to superior circuitry designs integrated by other local competitors and brands that imported technology from Taiwan and Japan. The TV manufacturing sector was highly competitive.

Upon thorough investigation, I discovered that their fundamental circuitry design was flawed, and they struggled to maintain quality control. Furthermore, their after-sales service left much to be desired. As a result, consumers were dissatisfied with the product, leading to a decline in market demand. People simply had no preference for this particular TV due to the issues with its design and quality. The management decided to gradually lower the production. However, we had an enormous stock of cabinets, raw materials like capacitors, resistors, and other electronic and mechanical components in large quantities, as we were supposed to supply them with *200 TV sets every ten days*, thus we were maintaining an inventory of the parts of the entire supply chain for their TV sets. The brand was on the downhill and within a year, its market hit rock bottom.

They had a big bureaucratic setup. The payments to partner suppliers like us started getting delayed. They had an extensive line of creditors and had to make huge payments to us. The C-forms attracted 4% CST on all sets and the accrued due payable to us was Rs. 40 Lakhs. This would be a substantial amount even today, but imagine the value of this sum in the decade of the 80s when this incident happened. It is equivalent to 7.5 crore in today's terms. *Lack of payment brought us under piles of debt.*

At times, life brings you to a crossroads where, despite your utmost efforts and good intentions, it presents roadblocks and setbacks. You find yourself chewing over what actions led to this situation. Does a divine presence even exist? Why does it seem like God is not favoring your side, especially when you believe you have harmed no one? Given the severity of the situation and the losses we had incurred, I approached the marketing director, who also happened to be a good friend from our college days, with great hope. While he offered assurances, they proved to be ineffective. It soon became apparent that he had left the company himself. Despite my desperation, I went to meet him in an attempt to gain insight into the company's internal affairs, but it did not yield substantial information.

The company was plagued by bureaucracy, management indecision, and delays caused by superiors, whether intentional or unintentional. Despite my persistent follow-ups, I kept receiving the same response that they were "looking into the matter." The attrition rate among senior-level employees was notably high.

In the meantime, I decided to reach out to Mrs. X, the wife of the owner, who was supposedly in charge of the business. To my surprise, she had no knowledge of the subject matter and was unaware that there were more than 50 suppliers of TVs and components to Nicky Tasha, at least that's the impression she gave. While she held a position on paper, in reality, she was clueless about the operations. This situation highlighted the common issue where women may hold positions but are often disconnected from the actual work, leading to a lack of credibility or perceptions of being overconfident. In light of this, I decided to bypass further discussions with her and speak directly to the owner.

The Persistent Effort

The amount of frustration and uneasiness I went through is unexplainable. I had a strong feeling if it was a man in my shoes, he would have handled it differently. This frustration went on mounting. The erupting tsunamis in my mind made me an insomniac.

I had made up my mind that I would get to the owner at any cost. I had to. I was responsible for so many workers and families who worked tirelessly to keep my operation running. I decided to visit Mr. X and tried to fix up an appointment. I called his residence and was informed that he was taking a shower, then I made several calls and I was told he had left for the factory and reached around 9:30 am. I had to speak to him and I decided to head there. I called my executive to accompany me. We reached the plant and, as anticipated, Mr. X had not yet arrived. He often visited that plant in the late hours. Therefore, we then drove to Plant 1 in Faridabad and were told we just missed him.

We then went to the other plant. Of course, we had many layers to cross. The receptionist did not allow us initially, but after great persistence, when I insisted that I spoke to him at home and that he asked us to come and meet at the factory; they sent us to the Private Secretary to the MD. When asked why I wanted to meet him, I felt very uneasy and decided not to explain her. I knew that if I had put the matter into words, she would have sent me to someone else to deal with the problem of money, and I would have gotten back into the loop. So I said, "We can explain only to Mr. X." The secretary said, "Mr. Nanda is busy in a meeting and won't be accessible till evening."

I remained resolute that we would not leave until we had the opportunity to meet Mr. X. The secretary recognized our determination. As noon arrived, there was still no sign of anyone emerging from the room where Mr. X was engaged. We returned to the Private Secretary once more, and she implored us to leave, explaining that it was challenging for Mr. X to meet us. However, I reiterated that we would not depart until we had a chance to meet with him, even if it meant waiting until he was available. My resolve remained set in stone.

Around 2 PM, Mr. X's meeting eventually concluded, and approximately 10-12 senior executives marched out of the room. Again, the secretary urged us to explain the problem to her so she could convey it to Mr. X on our behalf. However, I remained steadfast.

By 3 PM, we received the call to meet with Mr. X. His initial question was, "Why did you have to go through all this trouble just to meet me?" My response was straightforward: "I had no other choice. No one in your office was responding. If you do not settle my dues, I will not be able to clear my bills. In such a scenario, people may end up barging into my office, bypassing several security measures you have in place. They would not heed the receptionist or the manager. I might even have to surrender my office and relinquish my car keys, at the very least."Mr. X expressed his apologies and disclosed that he was going through a tough period. He described their challenging situation, including having lakhs of unsold stocks that they had procured, a tax liability of 7 lakhs against C-forms, and a 40 lakh credit with them. This put me under immense pressure. In an attempt to resolve the situation, he tried to persuade me to consider buying shares of their company due to their financial difficulties, and he presented his balance sheet.

Out of humanitarian considerations, I proposed a plan involving five installments to facilitate the payment process for him. I also insisted on receiving a C Form or an equivalent tax payment within the next three days. I meticulously maintained every detail related to C-forms, including all follow-up letters and comprehensive accounting information that might be needed. In a matter of days, we received all the C-forms, along with a check for 80,000 rupees, followed by another for 1 lakh rupees, ultimately totaling 7 lakhs. However, the payments came to a halt, and to make matters worse, the checks began to bounce due to insufficient funds.

It became apparent that even a prominent industry leader like Mr. X could not fulfill his commitments. Consequently, we had no choice but to pursue legal action and go to court. While it was still advantageous for them, many small industries like ours likely had to file cases against them. Unfortunately, the Indian legal system at that time was marked by numerous layers, which provided larger companies with opportunities to extend legal proceedings, buying time without having to make payments.

Meanwhile, smaller companies like ours accumulated more debt, effectively subsidizing the operations of these larger industries. It was truly disheartening. Despite persistent efforts and the government's recognition of the challenges faced by Small Scale Industries, a law was introduced stipulating that if post-dated cheques bounced, banks would take action on the defaulters' bank accounts and impose penalties. However, this law proved to be largely ineffective, as no major consequences followed.

Ultimately, we were left with no alternative but to pursue legal action by taking the cases to court.

Uptron - Going Strong

Our business relationship with Uptron India Ltd was thriving. They had five units located in Uttar Pradesh and Uttarakhand, including places like Bhimtal. As it was a state government project, payments were consistently smooth and reliable. Some vendors who supplied Uptron TVs were also sourcing tuners from us and purchasing complete TV sets featuring the Uptron logo. This collaboration continued until around the year 2003.

The Push with the Bush

The episode involving Bush India Ltd. is another intense memory that remains fresh in my mind. As the company encountered financial difficulties, they ceased communication with us. Fortunately, the outstanding amount was not exceptionally large, totaling around 4-5 lakhs. After engaging in conversations with them, we learned that Bush had shut down its operations and continued to function under a different name. When I finally managed to contact the person responsible, he openly admitted that Bush India had established a new company, but they had not transferred their creditors to that new entity. Consequently, they were unable to make payments any longer.

Economic Reformation- Changing Face of India

The year 1991 is etched into my memory as a pivotal moment that ignited economic reform in India. It marked the end of the

License Raj, a system that had long been a source of sluggish economic growth and corruption, crippling the Indian economy for decades. The economic reforms of 1991 were transformative in several ways:

- **Abolishing License Raj**: The most marked change was the elimination of licensing restrictions for almost all industries, with exceptions for 18 sectors related to security, strategic concerns, social reasons, safety, and overriding environmental issues.
- **Foreign Investment Incentives**: The reforms aimed to attract foreign investment by pre-approving investments with up to 51% foreign equity participation. This opened the doors for foreign companies to bring modern technology and industrial development to India.
- **Technological Advancement**: The policy of requiring government approval for foreign technology agreements was scrapped to encourage technological advancement.
- **Dismantling Public Monopolies**: The government initiated the process of privatization by floating shares of public sector companies. Public sector growth was limited to essential infrastructure, goods and services, mineral exploration, and defense manufacturing.
- **Abolishing MRTP**: The concept of Monopolies and Restrictive Trade Practices (MRTP) companies, where companies with assets exceeding a certain value were placed under government supervision, was eliminated.

These reforms liberalized the Indian economy, leading to a major acceleration of development. A new trade policy was introduced, emphasizing exports and the removal of import controls. It proposed limiting tariff rates to no more than 150 percent, reducing excise duties, and abolishing export subsidies. The country and its economy were undergoing a rapid and comprehensive transformation. Reference: *Economic liberalization in India (From Wikipedia)*

While the 1982 Asian Games, had already kick-started the entry of color television in India, at that time, at least 50,000 color televisions were being imported into the country **post-liberalization,** *there were a few companies that started importing almost 80 percent of components. Larger companies like Samtel and Videocon had set up sophisticated plants for picture tubes, which seemed more technically advanced and indigenous. The components were being imported mainly from 3 countries and 3 brands Lucky Gold Star, Samsung and ITT, about* "410 out of 450 components (required to make a color TV set)", were imported whereas *Certain components, such as picture tubes and integrated circuits, were manufactured in India at that time. (Suvam Pal is an independent media professional, author and documentary filmmaker.)*

(Courtesy: Sandeep Khanna, former Editor and Author)

The demand for televisions in India was experiencing exponential growth, even though only one or two television channels were available. I vividly remember the debut of "Hum Log," the first TV serial broadcast by Doordarshan, India's sole TV channel, in 1984. People were captivated by their television sets, eagerly awaiting each episode of Manohar Shyam Joshi's "Hum Log" or the weekly musical program "Chitrahar."

The television landscape underwent a pronounced transformation with the advent of cable television technology. Cable TV offered viewers a multitude of program choices and channels, largely boosting television viewership.

In February 1991, the Gulf War erupted, leading to an unprecedented surge in demand for cable TV. People were glued to their television screens to follow the Gulf War news coverage provided by CNN. Surprisingly, the demand for cable TV persisted even after the war ended.

In 1999, Star TV from Hong Kong revolutionized Indian television by launching multiple entertainment programs and aggressively marketing them to Indian viewers. Electronic media had rapidly become an essential part of every household's lifestyle.

Despite economic liberalization, the performance of the electronics hardware industry in terms of partial and total productivity remained underwhelming. Many firms preferred to import technology rather than invest in research and development to develop it domestically. The electronics landscape in the country was rapidly evolving due to several factors. Government policy changes, increased import of color televisions, and economic liberalization caused a surge of foreign brands in India. By 1995, the country was inundated with international brands.

Small-scale manufacturers faced intense competition from these international brands. While the demand for black and white televisions continued, it noticeably dwindled in urban cities as it was replaced by color televisions, which cost around Rs. 15,000. Consequently, people began selling their black and white televisions in the secondary market. This secondary market gained prominence among the urban lower-middle-class community.

India lagged in the development of electronic products; even tuners for color televisions were being imported from other countries.

Checkmate! Liberalization and Technological Advancement - Inverted U

The rapid technological advancements and economic liberalization greatly impacted the market for black and white TVs and related components. What had once experienced exponential growth took a sudden U-turn and plummeted, especially in urban and metropolitan cities. This shift brought about a multitude of challenges, including issues with existing vendors, mounting bad debts, the need for technological upgrades, a lack of technical competencies, and changes in market demands.

While I had initially focused on black-and-white TVs, I recognized the need to adapt to these changes. To address the evolving market, I obtained a license from the Ministry of Small-Scale Industry to manufacture color televisions. However, the path ahead was fraught with challenges, as the competition in the color TV market was intense. Even large players in the industry struggled and quickly succumbed to the pressures of the changing market. We found ourselves in a similar predicament, as all our investments had become obsolete, and scaling up to color TV technology seemed nearly impossible.

We had reached a dead end and were compelled to explore alternative avenues. During that period, there were two common methods of importing electronics: CKD (complete knockdown) and SKD (semi-knockdown), which encompassed various types of electronic goods. To navigate the changing tapestry, I decided to import two-in-one devices, which had a substantial demand in the country. The appeal of these devices was so widespread, that even a milkman would carry a small transistor while traveling from one village to another to deliver milk.

Radios served as a dominant source of entertainment in those days, and this venture proved lucrative for several years. The demand for these devices was akin to the widespread adoption of mobile technology in today's world. I had read that *'change is the only constant in life'.* I felt that the Almighty wanted to teach me its true meaning.

Despite numerous challenges, such as payment delays and debts, I persisted in TV manufacturing. However, the galloping influx of foreign investments into India and the intensifying competition posed by foreign television brands in the country were gradually shifting my focus from the domestic industry to the realm of exports. The export marketing course I attended in Finland in 1989 had already ignited a spark in me, and I began to see better prospects in the international market.

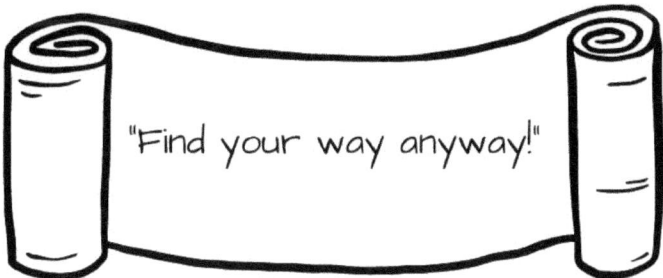

"Find your way anyway!"

Key Takeaways

- ✎ Take stock of your dreams, dig out ways to achieve them, and most importantly, develop a doer's mindset.
- ✎ No matter how big your dreams are, do not get intimidated. Just be mindful of how to eat an elephant: bit-by-bit. So, a step-by-step approach can inch you closer to your dreams. And dreams are meant to be accomplished!
- ✎ Prioritize supply chain integration to ensure high product quality.
- ✎ Actively involve yourself in organizing events for women entrepreneurs.
- ✎ Even if you are an entrepreneur, do not shy away from seeking training and learning the ropes of your product/s.
- ✎ When faced with issues like delayed payments, bureaucracy, and management issues, demonstrate persistence and determination.
- ✎ Be change-ready. Stay vigilant about market fluctuations and be prepared to pivot if needed.

CHAPTER 4

Global Stage – A Way Forward

"We cannot solve our problems with the same thinking we used when we created them."

– Albert Einstein

Way Forward the Purpose for Bigger Plunge

The events of life taught me the hard way that resilience is everything. I needed to move on and figure out something that would keep me afloat in the business scenario. That was my energy point and inspiration. I felt that the Almighty was throwing opportunities at me during my rugged days in television and electronics as if a plan for me was already in the making.

Searching for the right product, timing, and place is the only way forward for an entrepreneur. It is a continuous journey; failures act as bars that row the boat in the right direction. The international Market was opening up, and I decided to go beyond the boundaries of the country; in an era when there were rotary dials, no internet, no mobile phones, communication happened via landlines, and we had to book trunk calls to connect with anyone outside Delhi, it cost Rs. 100 a minute to make an international call, facsimile machines were the most modern way to communicate via letters. Receiving a faxed document was a big deal, as that meant an important global message had come through.

In 1989, I received an invitation to participate in another export training program organized by Prodec in Finland. This was my second trip abroad, with my first being a visit to Europe and the UK in 1982 as part of a delegation organized by the

National Alliance of Young Entrepreneurs. I eagerly accepted the opportunity to expand my knowledge of international markets, and I was filled with excitement.

Our group comprised women from South Asia and Southeast Asia, primarily representing SAARC (The South Asian Association for Regional Cooperation). There were 15 of us, each with different backgrounds, including a few from the government and others who were entrepreneurs from various countries. I was the sole Indian woman in the group. This trip provided me with valuable exposure to various products suitable for the international market. I gained in-depth knowledge about the export process, market surveys, and the right approach to export marketing.

1989 - Training at the Helsinki School of Economics on Export Marketing by PRODEC

Prepared but Not Perfect: International Marketing

The training program was intensive, and the classes were very informative; I learned different ways to analyze and understand international marketing and how to proceed once the product selection is made. International market research is an essential key to successful export planning. It was necessary to critically review and assess the demand for your products and factors related to your export destination. It will make the system more efficient concerning export plans, cost, and time schedules. I studied German markets for all my products.

It was a thorough study of marketing and exporting products to the European market, meeting the requirements of European buyers, pricing factors, trade information from the other countries, detailed know-how about customs tariffs of European countries, harmonized codes of the products, and customs tariffs of our own country. At that time in India, the import-export departments did not detail harmonized codes. Harmonized Systems (HS) of Nomenclature – are the codes used worldwide to categorize and identify different products.

Color trends that change from season to season and year to year; their requirements for festivals, holidays, and according to seasons were a part of the detailed curriculum. The industry experts in Helsinki imparted profound knowledge.

As a part of the program, we had the opportunity to visit different industries, garment designers, garment manufacturers, and some well-known places for design. It instilled a unique difference in my thought process. For the first time, I realized that my country needed to catch up on technology. Through these visits, I acquired a slew of experience regarding new ideas and products and exposure, the methods of pricing and costs analysis. And how one could introduce companies to European buyers, for example, through trade fairs or sales missions.

During our trip, we had the opportunity to visit **Marimekko, a renowned scarf** manufacturer. Marimekko had faced financial losses and was eventually sold to Kristi Paakanen, another entrepreneur. Kristi Paakanen successfully used innovative methods to revive the company, turning it into a success story. This experience taught me that if your business is not doing well, there is the possibility of selling it to a more successful entrepreneur at a better price. This buyout can happen because of the unique strengths of your company.

We also visited a children's school with a unique design, and the classrooms were filled with innovative creations. The school had a limited number of students, and they were taught art and engaged in remarkable creative experiments. It was an eye-opening experience to see children learning and experimenting at such an early age. This was in 1989.

Globalization presented numerous opportunities for India to leverage its demographic and economic potential. While there are many innovative schools in India today, back in 1989, we were still far from infusing innovation and skill development into schools. There were only a handful of such schools that offered admissions based on VIP quotas or to international students until around 2005.

Helsinki had the most fascinating weather. It was brimming with greenery and flowers around. The city was cold and beautiful. Helsinki was aesthetically pleasing, with its natural beauty of snow and flora. The sun's rays penetrated the clouds and remained till late evening. There was evening daylight from 2 AM. to 4 AM.; it was somewhat dark, not as dark as we have in India, but a shade of night. Then from 4 AM., the daylight would appear again. I was falling in love with the country more and more.

Possible Opportunities to Export

We visited a mega hypermarket retail outlet with 120 branches in the country, named Tammer-Tukku in Tampere, Finland, with a vast range of products, just like a Walmart in the USA or Big Bazaar in India. We learned the system of bar coding, packaging, transportation, logistics, and other details. That was an incredibly eye-opening and knowledge-gaining experience.

This store was sizable and had a huge variety of goods on the shelves. In 1989, India did not have an open economy, so there were no MNCs. The openings for innovations or new products could have been more extensive. And during such periods, this kind of exposure was altogether new and extraordinary. They even wanted items like soaps, detergents, towels, etc.

Management Practices

We had many eye-openers and contrasts in the business environment in India. It was amazing to learn that in the 80s, irrespective of your status, one should be reachable to their employees. There were no hierarchies, simply flat structures. While we interacted with the management, I found it difficult to differentiate the owner from the employee. We were surprised that the MD was already sitting amongst the employees and did not throw his weight around to show his presence. He was so inconspicuous.

Further, the owner was a part of the management, unlike the system in India, where ownership can be separated from the employees. The interaction between the Indian CEO and the employees often smells of superiority or inferiority. Only the MNC culture has now opened the doors of having lunch together at their restaurant or canteen, eating similar food with employees sitting around.

Secondly, employees were very relaxed and were not anxious about his presence. The culture of addressing everyone by their first name, to some extent, also probably removes the formality that exists in the Indian context. Tammer-Tukku had a standard canteen having a capacity of 450 to 500 people. Everyone was munching lunch in the same canteen with the bosses around, and there were no separate sections or rooms for the executives, a perfect example of egalitarian culture. Unless you asked for the designation, it was easier for a stranger or a visitor to identify the boss from the employees.

At that time, only a handful of IT companies in India interacting with MNCs in the USA or other countries followed this culture. But they still had a separate lunchroom for the Directors. A few adopted that, as all other organizations needed such a culture. It prevails even today. The owners take their lunch separately, or the Directors will bring it together, and employees will take it separately.

These experiences and the knowledge I gained provided valuable early insights and a deep understanding of international practices and cultures. Interacting with women from different countries broadened my perspective of cultural differences.

For instance, the women from Indonesia and Malaysia appeared to be more reserved and less expressive compared to women from other countries. One evening, I offered some snacks that I had brought from India, as buying them there could be expensive. Sharing snacks is a common practice in our country when in a group. However, this gesture made them feel uncomfortable. I realized that they felt insecure around strangers, and they tended to keep to themselves. They did not exchange smiles or greetings, not only with me but also among themselves. This was a cultural shock for them. While they might acknowledge soft attitudes and emotions internally, they were selective about expressing them.

Cultural differences are sizable, and they influence how products are designed and marketed. For instance, Western societies are often more individualistic, with weaker ties to families and social groups. In contrast, Indian culture tends to prioritize the needs of the group. British people, for example, are less likely to sacrifice their personal needs for the group, as mentioned by Hugo Messer in his book "How to Overcome Cultural Differences when Managing Offshore or Nearshore Teams". Hugo Messer is a Dutch entrepreneur, distributed agile team specialist, and author. Understanding these cultural nuances is vital for successful marketing and product development.

I once had an interesting experience while traveling from Cologne to Hamburg. I shared a train compartment with a German lady. Despite our language barrier, we exchanged greetings through our glances. As the journey progressed, we managed to communicate and get to know each other better. By the time we reached our destination, we had learned about each other's families and various other things, even though we could not have a full conversation due to our language differences.

During a delegation trip to Kyrgyzstan with 15 women entrepreneurs for an exhibition, I had another fascinating cultural encounter. We had partnered with an organization based in

Kyrgyzstan, and they organized a gala dinner for all the delegates. While sitting on the dais with the president of the organization, I noticed that many women at the event were putting dry fruits, chicken, and fruits in polythene bags. I found this quite strange and initially felt that it was a bit impractical.

However, a few minutes later, when we started eating, I picked up my plate and found a similar bag under it. I then learned that this practice was rooted in their pastoral nomadic lifestyle, and it was a way to prevent food waste. These women were highly conscious about not wasting food, as they had historically lived by hunting and always carried their food with them. It was a valuable lesson in cultural understanding and respect for their traditions.

I was not trying to judge any country or culture during my international experiences; instead, I was focused on forming perceptions and understanding differences, which I believed to be key in international business. Throughout my journey, I made terrific friends from countries like Bangladesh, Bhutan (Phub Zam), and Nepal (Shanti Chadha). We eventually returned to our respective countries.

As I continued to grapple with the electronics industry for an extended period, I faced a crossroads. I had to contemplate whether to persist in this direction or explore alternative paths. It was a landmark question mark for me, especially as I found myself at a clear competitive disadvantage compared to the major players in the industry. By 1992, global partnerships and tie-ups were becoming common for large manufacturers and international brands in this rapidly changing technological landscape. Given the nature of electronics as a fast-evolving industry, I recognized the need for substantial investments to compete with global giants.

Recognizing the need for a fresh start and realizing that I had to move forward, I decided to reset and restart my business. The burgeoning global economy in India motivated me to shift my focus toward more weighty export endeavors. Armed with a basic understanding of international marketing principles from my previous experiences, I established an export company named **'Shree Ganpati Exports'** in 1992. The intent was to export to USA and Germany.

To facilitate this transition, I obtained an Importer-Exporter Code (IEC) from the Directorate General of Foreign Trade (DGFT) and a Permanent Account Number (PAN) from the Income Tax Department. The policies introduced in 1991 played a pivotal role in encouraging export houses and trading houses to import various items. The government also facilitated the establishment of trading companies with up to 51 percent foreign equity to promote exports. Furthermore, the 1994-95 policy introduced a new category of trading houses known as Super Star Trading Houses. These policy changes provided the necessary framework for my export-focused business to thrive.

In 1992, I had the opportunity to go on another trip, this time to the Netherlands. I participated in a four-week training program organized by CBI, the Center for the Promotion of Imports from developing countries, based in Rotterdam. Through this training, I sought to amplify my knowledge of exports and understand how to access data and research on the various products required by European countries.

1992 - Training on Export Marketing at CBI, Rotterdam, Netherlands

Nowadays, we can readily access export and import data through digital systems. However, during that time, obtaining import and export statistics instantly was not as straightforward, and this training helped bridge that knowledge gap.

The training at CBI was particularly beneficial for regions, especially those targeting the European market. It provided valuable acumen into what products were being imported from India, the quantities involved, and product-wise data for specific years. This empowered us to make informed decisions regarding our export endeavors.

The country's economy still needed to be opened. Then, after a year, Prodec invited the same group of women entrepreneurs to take up marketing management for the second time as part of phase two. This time, the group was called to Amsterdam, and the training took place with the CBI (Center for the Promotion of Imports) of the Netherlands at Rotterdam. We all met there again. The training was for about 15 days. The schedule was very tight. Their objective was to help small and medium-sized enterprises (SMEs) strengthen their economic, social, and environmental sustainability; by enabling complementary economies to export products and services to Europe and regional markets.

After completing the training, everybody was supposed to research some subject and write down the market details and outcomes. Each of us had to write a project on different themes, depending on our country-wide selection of products. We were supposed to study the country's resources, raw material and demand pattern, consumption pattern, and local availability and competition with other countries. We had to select one European country. I had selected Germany – 3 others had also chosen Germany. My interaction with them was pretty limited. We had decided on a particular agency in Germany to interact with and approach other agencies to collect the data. As a part of the itinerary, we had to review the market and explore people's buying habits and the stores that catered to the needs of different segments of society. I used to get many compliments for being efficient and always on time for all my meetings for my research study.

My project was to study the German Market and its requirements for "*Cotton Garments in Germany and export potential from India to Germany.*" It was hinged on a thorough market study based on detailed parameters of the Indian origin of cotton versus demand in Germany and Europe. I also took into account their buying and selling patterns based on consumer behaviors, and keynote and factual information. So I also got to research cotton consumption in India versus Germany. *It was my first research paper published and circulated in Europe and other institutions.*

While studying export marketing, I learned that for effective marketing, I must know the exact nature of the market, whether it is cotton fabric choice, bend, sizes, floral or abstract prints, and products. This knowledge makes stepping into the Market and selling the product feasible.

People visit and pick up a few souvenirs from India, and it is presumed that this product has demand in that country; this is a big misconception. Whatever people buy as a souvenir is not the correct market assessment.

With starry eyes, a person packed a suitcase with fresh night suits and flew to Europe to sell those. But to his dismay, there was no market for night suits in Europe. He found that European people generally do not sleep with night suits on. So, this was a piece of great information to learn.

We visited Utrecht Mart, located about 50 kilometers from the city. It was a wholesale market for all kinds of goods, from leather goods to jewelry, clothing, body care accessories, home furnishing, beauty products, pearls, semi-precious stones, etc. All the importers and retailers would go to this Market to buy their stocks. We went around and got good exposure to the Market. At that time, I wished we also had a similar market in our country.

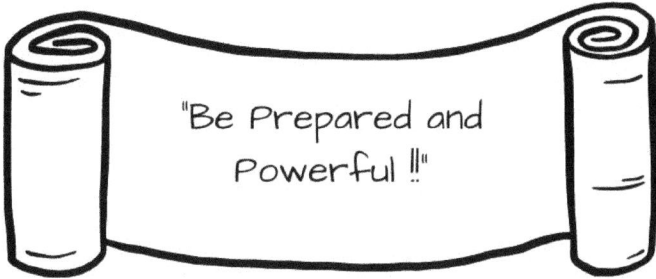

"Be Prepared and Powerful !!"

Cultural and Buying Eco-System Differences: In fashion, home decor, and various other industries, seasonal colors play an exceptional role. Different regions and countries have their color preferences based on cultural, climate, and seasonal factors.

It was an eye-opener to experience cultural differences and buying patterns. I had the opportunity to study the buying behaviors in the retail space in Germany. Some malls were very expensive, some were moderate, and some were cheap. After visiting them 2-3 times and comparing the prices, it was interesting to see the data of the people who were coming there for shopping and then visiting the buying offices of these stores.

The people of Germany had very typical buying habits. Women and men who were extremely busy would go to a specific store with high-end products and pick the most expensive products. German brands like C&A, H&M, and KiK focus on consumers who rarely buy under the influence of emotions. Apart from the German-language website, a store chosen by the client should provide a product of stable quality at a price that goes hand in hand with it. If the brand meets Germans' expectations, they will remain faithful to it for a long time. German brands that have succeeded internationally are only a confirmation of the Germans' ideals – high quality and fair price.

When I went to the second store, surprisingly, similar products were available at a slightly lower price. In the third category store, some products were quite the same, some with a marginal difference, but the cost of the similar products was cheaper than in the middle segment store. So, the same product in 3 types of stores had a different price range.

After discussing with them, I found that people need more time or the habit of going around stores or doing window shopping. They were not habitual in window shopping, So; the purchase companies would keep similar products with different prices for different segments of buyers.

Thirdly, the Buying company's procurement company was vending from 4-5 stores and had buying offices in Hong Kong. They were given the fresh indent to buy collectively and then do the distribution accordingly. That was known as the central purchasing system, which increased the profit of all stores. Cheaper goods, like lingerie and undergarments, were only found in the cheap-priced stores, and as the buyer would not move from one store to another, it made no difference to them. This market research gave me a new perspective.

There were a lot of companies from India that had opened offices in Frankfurt. They either collaborated with German companies or had German goods in their offices. Banaras House was one of those I visited, though; finally, nothing could be materialized with them. After some time, we returned to our respective countries after submitting the research papers.

During this period, I focused on leather goods based on the demand within India. I conducted surveys and engaged in conversations with companies interested in leather products. While attending classes on "how to explore the export market," I would seize opportunities to step out, make phone calls, and arrange meetings with potential clients. This proactive approach helped me secure a few leads, and they expressed their willingness to visit Delhi, India, or engage in correspondence regarding the desired products. Once I returned to India, I carefully reviewed the list of important companies and initiated communication with them. This method allowed me to generate leads for the export business. We must conduct thorough market research and analyze consumer behavior to identify emerging trends and tailor our export strategy accordingly.

The product portfolio included a wide array of leather products, ladies' purses, bags, wallets, executive folders, credit card holders, cigar holders, etc. I was determined to provide excellence in quality. However, I needed help to find quality raw materials for the products in India, which I saw in USA or European countries. Even the accessories were not available. In these countries, there were very decorative items as accessories for ladies, like bags, purses, etc. So finally, I took products like portfolios, backpacks, diaries, wallets, and cosmetic bags meant for men or office use.

There was an upcoming leather fair in Hong Kong where I decided to participate and have my stall to showcase my products. So, I prepared the products for that event. I knew well that I did not have much knowledge about the subject. So I visited tanneries in Calcutta (now known as Kolkata), Kanpur, and Agra. I acquired loads of technical know-how on quality, finish, and designs.

On the first day of the fair in Hong Kong, I did not get any orders. I was very disheartened but stood firm. The next day, I met a company based in China having an office in Hong Kong. I got the first order from them, and that also, straight for three containers of leather cut pieces of 3 inches. The wastage from leather garments and products was procured and exported, at least 3-4 containers every month. It was real hard work. I had to ensure I was sending the right quality, correct sizes, and usable waste. It was challenging and worth the return. My team worked well. This Chinese buyer was staying in Hong Kong but had a factory in Guangzhou, China. and insisted I visit his factory in China and sign a bigger deal.

1998 - Exhibition of Handicrafts at Bratislava, Slovakia,
(then Czechoslovakia), with the organizer

Germany was another country I focused on. The IGEP in India and the German Ministry of Economic Cooperation and Development (BMZ) helped the leather exporters from India to Germany.

Exporting goods from India presented a multitude of challenges. It required strict adherence to guidelines, including customs procedures, declarations, packaging specifications, logistics coordination, labeling, quality standards, product samples, production considerations, and credit matters. These complexities necessitated careful attention and expertise to navigate the international export landscape successfully.

Exporting products to international markets requires a keen understanding of future consumer needs and preferences. Anticipating trends and emerging demands in various regions can give your business a competitive edge.

1998 - Exhibition of Handicrafts at Bratislava, Slovakia,
with the buyers on the left and right

Adaptability and Innovation

The global market is ever-changing, and being adaptable to evolving trends and demands is essential. Continuously innovating your products, processes, and marketing strategies will help you maintain a competitive edge in the export market.

Once, a buyer from Vienna got me in great trouble by not accepting our Letter of Credit due to a difference of opinion between the two partners in Vienna, and a critical amount of payment got stuck with them. Generally, against the Letter of Credit, you send the Bill of Lading along with the other documents to release the goods. They did not release the goods, there was demurrage being incurred, and I felt the pinch of going through losses. After ten days, I decided to visit Hamburg to settle the matter. My son, who was 20 years old, accompanied me. It was a learning experience for him. From the Hamburg port, the goods used to go to Vienna by truck.

1999 - Visiting Salzburg, Austria at a Buyer Meet

One person at the Hamburg port helped me a lot to release all the goods, and I made great efforts to sell all the goods to different buyers. At least, this minimized losses, and I could meet the demurrage charges levied in the shipment due to the late release of goods, and I was left with a marginal profit.

One has to be alert and handle such kinds of buyers. Generally, one ensures the material will be released on the letter of credit. But I just learned that the differences between the two partners would create difficulties for suppliers like us. But I wish I had understood that. It was pretty unpredictable.

That experience and training set a reason and zeal to further explore markets for other products. So, I also decided to take up Silver Jewelry, Sterling Silver Reena D. The purity of Silver had to be 92.25 for export. I used to procure silver jewelry from Jaipur and got some items manufactured in Delhi—their obvious stipulation for silver jewelry. I did my designs. Certain chemicals were not allowed doing Silver plating as they did not suit their skins. The authorities had laid down the specifications; this was again a herculean challenge to train my mind on the export products. Meeting international quality standards and regulatory requirements is crucial for export success. Different countries may have specific regulations and certifications that your products must adhere to. Ensuring your products meet these standards demonstrates professionalism and reliability, which are essential for building a strong export business.

1999 - Personal Networking with my Buyer from Sweden
- Visiting her at her residence with a warm, memorable welcome!

I have visited Europe and the USA, and now have many connections there. Of course, I was open to the idea that whatever came as a demand for export, I would take it up. And whatever order I got, I would fulfill it.

I ventured into the home furnishing business with a German buyer. What fascinated me was his in-depth knowledge of the Indian market. He could effortlessly list the products available on specific streets or in particular shops, along with details about the manufacturers and the city in India. His primary focus was on adding value to these products to meet the demands of the German market. His expertise and attention to detail left me thoroughly impressed.

Seasonal colors hold great significance in industries, such as fashion and home decor. Preferences for colors vary among different regions and countries, influenced by cultural, climatic, and seasonal factors. Adapting your product designs and color schemes to resonate with the seasonal trends in your target markets can enhance the appeal of your products and contribute to their market success. This approach allows you to cater to the unique preferences of diverse consumer segments around the world.

My experience in the USA taught me that buyers prefer focused purchases rather than a wide variety of samples. Providing seven to ten samples with different color combinations in related product categories is more appealing. For instance, offering a bedcover with matching cushions, pillows, table covers, towels, napkins, dining table covers, and coffee table covers in a cohesive color family is a strategic approach with one story line... Additionally, including matching wooden napkin rings and candle stands can be enticing.

Dealing with Italian buyers was more challenging for me. They tended to confirm orders but delayed payments, sometimes up to 60 days. Fortunately, we had insurance coverage for such situations, but it still presented complications and added a level of frustration to the process.

Such experiences create a divide, and you must be careful when dealing with some European countries. Exports demand a forward-looking approach that takes into account futuristic demands, seasonal colors, and trends. Staying informed, culturally sensitive, and agile in response to market changes will position your export business for success in the international arena.

As a part of my expansion, I started a company based in the USA, in St. Louis, Missouri. I made it an importing office cum warehouse to receive the goods ordered and sold to retailers. We appointed agents and salespersons in the USA who would visit and get the requirements of different retailers and connect with their head office for the requirements and supplies. Continuous sampling and further product development was done depending on the needs and orders. My son was instrumental in this expansion. The USA was a massive market. China was the biggest competitor, and its pricing was aggressive. We identified retail spaces and marts in their leading retail malls for the leather and silver jewelry market. It was during Christmas, and the response was out of bounds. It was focused on commitment, and it enabled us to expand rapidly. Efficient logistics and a robust supply chain are vital for successful exports. Careful planning and coordination are necessary to manage inventory, transportation, and customs procedures effectively.

I have had numerous experiences, some disheartening, some thrilling. On the way, I met various types of people, dealt with very different situations, and, in the process, experienced life in the most varied ways, adding to the richness and plethora of life learnings.

I have always had a curious and creative mindset. I loved the richness of the canvas and wondered what the artists expressed and how I perceived their work. My passion for art led me to establish an Indian Contemporary Art Gallery, Art Elements, in the Hauz Khas Village, New Delhi alleys. It was a very happening place; people visited it for food, to shop for high-quality clothes and artifacts, and to hang around. I met several artists from Hyderabad and Udaipur and visited Shantiniketan, an art hub. We put up art exhibitions and shows at different places and indulged in auctions of prestigious art pieces from auction houses like Sotheby's and Christie's.

Entrepreneurship is 24x7, 365 Days Commitment

When navigating the ship of your business, you may bump into several high and low tides. There could be financial calculations that may need correction. Managing may look easy initially, but then it may turn irksome and leave you stumbling. And the list goes on. However, during my journey as an entrepreneur, I have learned one thing; if I have to succeed, I better keep moving forward, irrespective of all the crafty and rough routes I must take to reach my goal of success. The business demands dedication 24/7, 365 days.

However, once you decide to be unstoppable, the first prerequisite is to work on your beliefs. If your belief system needs to be corrected, no matter how determined you are, success may remain in distant quarters. In a nutshell, your beliefs are the vehicle that can accelerate you or repulse you from your desired success. Therefore, I identified 20 toxic beliefs holding me back, and I decided to replace those with 20 positive ones. That may sound easy, but believe me, it takes consistent effort. Therefore, I scribbled my 20 destructive beliefs and replaced them with 20 constructive ones.

For example, when I started my business, I was apprehensive about whether I would be a successful businesswoman. I dwelled on the belief 'I may or may not succeed.' So, I replaced this with 'Success is my birthright; I will succeed in whatever I set my belief on.'

I began a daily practice of writing down my newly formed beliefs. By repeatedly writing these positive affirmations each morning, they became ingrained in me. This practice allowed these affirmations to manifest in my thought processes and become an integral part of my body and mind. The transformation that this practice brought about was truly astonishing and rewarding. It rejuvenates you.

My Future Steps and Assessment

According to the Sixth Economic Census, women constitute around 14% of the total entrepreneur base in India, i.e., 8.05

million out of the real 58.5 million entrepreneurs. The number of females has increased almost three times in the UK, two times in the US and India. Even today, most women are in small-scale businesses. Thanks to digitization, the doors are now opening for all entrepreneurs, including women. Many women working in high posts have bid goodbye to the corporate world and marched into entrepreneurship for economic freedom. They want to turn the available time into a good account per their requirements and comforts.

However, finance, marketing, and venture capital have become areas where they often struggleand need help to cope. Albeit, there have been women who have struck it big. Kiran Mazumdar of Biocon, Anu Aga of Thermax, and S. Mallika Srinivasan of Tractors and Farm Equipment are a few who have crossed the 1 million mark. How could they do so? How could they triumph over the issues?

The past decade has seen an explosion of women starting businesses. Today, business tools are more readily accessible than when I started the business. Emerging entrepreneurs want to solve problems in new ways and see the success of peers who took the company from zero to millions in revenue in a few years. And yet, I worry. Where will women be, who are starting their businesses, in the next 5 to 7 years? Most women remain small-scale entrepreneurs or shut down their businesses due to a lack of marketing or funds. I aspire to help women raise capital, taking their thinking to the out-of-the-box level to solve their problems. I am passionate about helping more women build their businesses successfully.

A few outstanding women who proved themselves, like **Katharine Graham**, became the CEO of The Washington Post Company in 1972, making her the first female CEO of a Fortune 500 company. In her memoir, Graham outlines the personal struggles of a woman in such a high position at a publishing company. She constantly doubted herself and would often look for reassurance from male colleagues. Nevertheless, Graham played an integral part in the success of the Washington Post. During her three decades of leadership, revenue grew nearly twentyfold, and the Washington Post became a public corporation listed on the New York Stock Exchange.

I am a firm believer in 'Fortune favors the brave.' Anita Roddick said many business decisions came through circumstances and good luck rather than any prepared plan. The Body Shops' simple ethical message and promoting ethical and environmentally friendly consumerism helped grow a powerful brand image.

Anita Roddick talks of the ethos behind the Body Shop:

"We made a list of all the things we didn't want to be. We did not want to be these captains of industry. That didn't make our blood sing. I didn't want to be a cosmetic diva wearing high heels and make-up, prancing at celebrity functions. We were rooted in family and community."

While luck and circumstances can have an impact on business success, remember that they should not be the sole determinants of decision-making. Successful businesses place a strong emphasis on strategic planning, market research, risk assessment, and other proactive measures to enhance their likelihood of success. The combination of preparedness and the capacity to adapt to evolving circumstances is often the formula for achieving sustainable growth and long-term success.

Lessons Learned

Delegate

Research suggests that business revolves around people. One major misconception that can hinder your progress is the belief that you know everything and can handle everything most efficiently. To elevate your company to a million-dollar business, you should steer clear of this mindset. Leaders should set goals and lead their teams in achieving those goals, and this necessitates having an effective team in place. Regardless of the allure of technological advancements, business and industry are fundamentally driven by people, and for the benefit of people. People with business education might have the knowledge to manage personnel, handle finances, and lead senior management. However, it is a fallacy to think that is enough. Whether you are managing one person or a group of hundreds, the ability to relate to people is essential for the smooth operation of your organization. Fair and empathetic leadership is numero uno when dealing with people.

Effectiveness

Survival often depends on more than just how much effort we pour in but on whether the actions are in place in the proper direction. The correct development process occurs in every industry first, through leadership and second, through management.

If, as a leader in the industry, we do not keep navigating in the right direction, monitor the environment, and guide our team; expert management cannot lead anywhere except to failure.

Each degree of management success can only compensate for failure in leadership. Therefore, for effective management, the administration has to be equally effective.

Let's say the boss is on a business tour, and no one in the back office can do his job. He has kept everything to himself. He has plenty of men under him who are anxious to take on some of his work. But the boss needs to be made aware of this beautiful tool called delegation. No wonder this boss would be a poor leader and fail to manage things in the near and far future.

Create sustainable pillars of support

Asking for support does not make you small. I have found these traits present in us, in women, but not so prevalent in men. They will not ask even if they need it most. Most of us try to be the jack of all trades, which can hold us back. We are clear that we are the creator, the champion, and the visionary, but we should also know that we need to hire people more intelligent than us in certain areas of our business. We must employ advisors and coaches in finance, sales, and online/offline marketing to strategize our business.

Who is the greatest asset to the company? Well, it is none other than you. Why not spend some money to seek targeted training in specific areas?

We may think we will hire coaches when we have more money. But once you decide to scale up your business, this training schedule should be a part of your budget from the initial stage. Finding good advisors may take time, but one can work around this.

Creating a board of good advisors plays a crucial role. As we did in the Federation of Indian Women Entrepreneurs (FIWE) for non-profits, it is easy to get dedicated board members to help you generate funds, profits, and social activity. But for revenue, it could be taxing to get people on the board who will come forward rolling up their sleeves and help you find the right source of raw material or workforce.

We should forage for board members ready to invest their time and help us get things done. These five to eight members should be industry experts. These can be retired CEOs who are willing to help you forward.

We must seek support amongst our group of entrepreneur friends, for example, FIWE (Federation of Indian Women Group), or help others. These friends can help accelerate the growth of the company. Besides working all the time, worrying, and getting exhausted, we could remind each other that we have to focus more on creating strategies and systems rather than working doggedly. I encourage you to follow these disciplines.

Women may often feel drained and distracted as they juggle family responsibilities. However, remember that we should not fixate on seeking recognition for every action we take. Instead, we should emulate what men have been doing for generations: thinking ambitiously, presenting their ideas with confidence, and telling their stories persuasively and forcefully.

Situations Where my Inner Voice Stopped me from Doing Something

I got an export order through the exhibition in Hong Kong to export leather waste to China. Though the show was for leather goods and garments, the buyer ordered leather cut pieces after seeing a few of our leather goods made from leather waste. His requirement was huge, and he wanted 5-7 monthly containers.

I was excited. After reaching back, we sent two consignments to them in one month. As the buyer wanted more varieties, the buyer invited me to come to China so that he could show me the types of waste and sizes required for leather-cut waste. He made all the arrangements for my pick up from Hong Kong airport and visit to the factory, plus my stay in Zhongshan City, south of the Pearl River Delta in Guangdong province. He offered to take me around to show me some prominent places.

My inner voice advised me to bring my husband along, but he was occupied with work and encouraged me to go alone. Although I had visited Hong Kong and other Asia-Pacific countries before, China was new to me. I was not afraid of traveling, but I preferred my husband's company, so I postponed the trip multiple times.

Unfortunately, I could not visit, and as a result, I lost the order and the buyer, which had sizeable consequences for my business. This situation left me feeling terrible about myself, my husband, and my missed opportunity.

How have such situations affected me?

This situation jeopardized my future orders with the party. I lost a major customer and a valuable contact in that country. I felt deeply disappointed in myself and, of course, my husband.

I questioned why I could not summon the courage and confidence to travel to that country alone. Using the excuse of needing company on the trip hindered my business prospects and diminished the potential for future significant success.

How could I reframe my references in such situations?

I would go on the first instance to finalize the deal with the Chinese company, as this is the best opportunity I have got through the exhibition.

Why should I try to postpone due to unknown reasons unnecessarily? I should visit the same buyer and create new leads in the big marketplace of China.

I will not lose time anymore. I will muster the courage to move forward, not limit my potential, and there are no limiting factors.

I am not alone; I am with myself. There is nothing that I cannot do.

Key Takeaways

- ♭ Resilience and entrepreneurship form a great alliance.
- ♭ Exploring international markets for business growth. Learn about different industries, market trends, and cultural nuances.
- ♭ Understanding the local market and having a robust supply chain contributes to success.
- ♭ Always have risk management and contingency plans in place to deal with payment delays.
- ♭ The power of positive affirmations and self-belief can make your entrepreneurial venture more rewarding.
- ♭ Stay committed to consistent learning, whether about products or market dynamics. This showcases a growth-oriented mindset; a must-have for long-term success.
- ♭ Effective leadership involves delegating; empowering and trusting your team.
- ♭ Building a network of advisors and mentors is valuable. Collaboration and seeking support contribute to business growth.
- ♭ The distinction between leadership and management is insightful. Both are vital for organizational success, and effective management relies on strong leadership.
- ♭ Help women entrepreneurs triumph over roadblocks.
- ♭ Strategic planning and proactive measures align with the principles of sustainable business growth.
- ♭ Do not let fear or uncertainty cloud business opportunities.

✥ Learning from missed chances and using them as motivation for future endeavors is a positive approach.

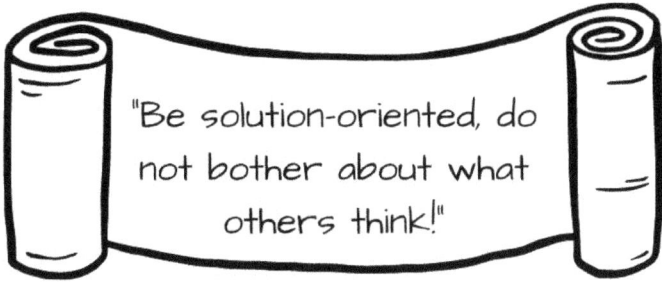

"Be solution-oriented, do not bother about what others think!"

CHAPTER 5

The Art of Fundraising

"Money is a reward for solving problems."

– Mike Murdock

Inadequate funding and a scarcity of capital are among the primary factors contributing to the failure of SME businesses. Business owners are acutely aware of the financial requirements necessary for the day-to-day operations of their companies, including payroll, fixed and variable overhead expenses like rent and utilities, and timely vendor payments. However, managing customer receivables can become challenging, particularly when operating on 60-day credit terms, with payments sometimes arriving after 90 or 120 days. This situation can disrupt financial calculations. Hence, you must strike a balance between receivables of 60 days and 120 days while incorporating this consideration into your financial planning and business strategy. Each project comes with unique financial needs. By doing so, you can prevent a gradual depletion of funds that might eventually jeopardize the existence of a small business.

Moreover, both women and men should be well-versed in financial management principles to drive success in their respective industries and thrive in the market. As I entered the TV business, there were other Asian competitors due to the substantial demand for televisions in the country. However, over time, these competitors faded away due to their lack of funds and their constant need for substantial credit facilities to distribute their products through dealers. This illustrates that while money is not the sole determinant of entrepreneurial success, it is imperative in the form of funds to execute a business plan effectively. In India, many women tend to hesitate when it comes to seeking financial support.

Entrepreneurship inherently involves risk, and there is a common perception that women are more risk-averse. This bias can be observed in the experiences of successful women entrepreneurs like Kiran Mazumdar-Shaw, who faced the "high-risk" label from potential investors when seeking funding for her biotechnology company, Biocon. Stereotypes also manifest in the fact that fewer women actively approach investors and are more reluctant to divest stakes, as reported by one interviewee (March 22, 2019, Bangalore).

When women do approach investors, they often face different perceptions compared to men. It has been noted that investors tend to prefer pitches presented by men, even when the content is identical. Additionally, challenges in obtaining funding are further exacerbated in India because women typically have limited property ownership, which can be used as collateral for loans. Around 79 percent of women-owned ventures are self-financed. However, families may still be hesitant to provide financial support to their daughters' entrepreneurial endeavors.

Fund Raising - Fears and Hesitation

Anjali Khanna, a jewelry manufacturer I met at the Pragati Maidan trade exhibition grounds in Delhi after a long time, had been involved in the business for quite a while. At that time, her children were young, and her husband was running an engineering unit.

During our conversation about various business aspects and market dynamics, I inquired, "How are you planning to manage your finances?" Anjali paused briefly, as if the question had caught her off guard, and then responded, "The product has enormous potential, and I've received positive feedback." However, I am not willing to take the risk of seeking funding from a bank. It involves a lot of paperwork, planning, and financial projections, and I am already very pressed for time. I cannot manage those formalities. My plan is to open a small boutique near my home."

She also mentioned in a hushed tone that she intended to use her savings. I suggested asking for financial assistance from her family and a few friends, but she was hesitant, concerned about whether they would be willing to lend to her. This unease in seeking funds is a common challenge faced by many women entrepreneurs.

After a lengthy discussion and our meetings, Anjali promised to seriously try fundraising for her business growth through her family and friends first. Then she will push for an outside loan.

This fundraising hesitation is widespread among women entrepreneurs. This is one substantial reason women often do not consider scaling up their businesses.

The modern women have started to un-snooze their true potential. They excel in every sphere of life, including business, politics, sports, entertainment, literature, and technology. Women are actively contributing to creating a more inclusive and evolved entrepreneurial ecosystem. In this context, financial knowledge becomes a high priority, helping them rise above the challenges and seize opportunities effectively.

Financially knowledgeable women make independent decisions in all aspects of life. They empower women to gain greater control over their lives, enhance their self-esteem, and provide them with an equal standing in family and community decision-making.

Handling Bad Debts and Bankrupt Creditors

I would like to recount a challenging experience from the folder of my experience when I supplied materials worth 40 lakhs to a dealer in Srinagar. Unfortunately, this dealer vanished without returning my calls, leaving me in a difficult situation. Another dealer offered reassuring promises but also faced bankruptcy. The ordeal became so severe that creditors would visit my office, demanding their payments and cautioning me about the consequences of further supplies of goods. Handling bad debts and bankrupt creditors can be a complex and herculean process.

Use this experience as a lesson for improving your credit management policies and risk assessment. Avoid making the same mistakes in the future. Managing bad debts and dealing with bankrupt creditors is a part of doing business. So, seek professional guidance when necessary and take proactive steps to minimize such situations in the future.

Ms. Anjana Tandon, Deputy General Manager, State Bank of India

Anjana Tandon presently works as Deputy General Manager at the State Bank of India. She joined the bank as a probationary officer and has held multiple assignments, including a stint in Singapore, in a career spanning more than 26 years. In her current role, she oversees the administrative office, which includes 167 branches in Gurugram, Faridabad, Sonipat, Palwal, and Mewat. She enjoys her role as a banker, as it provides her with an opportunity to meet people from diverse backgrounds.

How do women approach their loans? What is your perspective and experience of women entrepreneurs?

Women entrepreneurs are generally confident, creative, and skilled at multitasking. They have a strong desire to do something unique while also taking on family responsibilities. They are always willing to go the extra mile and are keen to create a positive impact. An increasing number of women are gaining financial independence and making their own decisions.

Can you share your experience as a banker and working with women entrepreneurs?

I have been in the banking profession for nearly 27 years and have had the privilege of interacting with a diverse range of customers and exploring various fields. Working with women entrepreneurs has always been a smooth experience because they are open and forthcoming. As a woman myself, I can relate to the nuances associated with their work.

Have you noticed any differences in how women entrepreneurs approach the loan process compared to their male counterparts?

They focus a lot on details and are keen to get things right in the first instance itself. They tend to be meticulous in their loan applications, paying close attention to every aspect of the process. This attention to detail reflects their determination to present a comprehensive and well-prepared application.

Furthermore, women entrepreneurs are generally more proactive in seeking guidance and assistance to ensure the success of their loan applications. They are eager to understand the specific requirements and procedures involved in securing a loan, and they are more likely to seek advice from financial experts and mentors to navigate the process effectively.

Do you think entrepreneurship is the right fit for women?

Women are increasingly making a mark in entrepreneurial ventures. Keeping in mind the specific business funding needs of women, banks offer customized schemes uniquely designed for them. For example, the State Bank of India offers the Stree Shakti Package for female entrepreneurs.

How about networking and building relationships with women entrepreneurs? Do you think these play a role in the loan process?

Networking today is essential to explore new opportunities, ideate and expand business. Having a network to share knowledge, information and resources could certainly open new channels/avenues for financing.

What advice would you give to women entrepreneurs who are considering applying for a business loan?

Having a comprehensive understanding of your business plan and its operational aspects is of utmost importance. Equally critical is knowing the right time to apply for a bank loan. Timely submission of all the necessary documents related to your entrepreneurial venture will expedite the loan approval process.

Monitoring your credit score is cardinal because a good credit history plays a pivotal role in the loan assessment. Furthermore, maintaining an open and transparent conversation with your banker regarding your future plans is highly advisable. This ensures that the bank can better support your business goals and financial needs.

Do you have any suggestions for aspiring women entrepreneurs?

Angel investors and venture capital funds are common types of investors in early-stage companies. Banks, however, are also an avenue for providing financial assistance in all stages of the business cycle. Women entrepreneurs can avail of a term loan, working capital loan or asset-backed loan based on their requirements.

Lack of Capital - Available Options

Capital can have long-term repercussions on your business. Having completed a short financial management course, I found it immensely helpful in deciphering financial complexities. While mastery does not happen overnight, it gradually equips you with a deeper understanding of financial intricacies and the language of finance. For women, developing robust financial skills is crucial.

Money can play an essential role in a business to success, but it cannot be the only reason for entrepreneurs to fail. There are thousands of businesses, and **business is like grass**; you feed it with water daily and see it grow. You can start with $0, but if you want it to grow faster than usual, you will need knowledge to invest and capital to realize your vision.

Access to Finance - It has been observed that women entrepreneurs face greater challenges when starting and managing businesses compared to their male counterparts. These experiences often discourage more women from entering the entrepreneurial arena, creating a self-perpetuating cycle. To break this cycle, women entrepreneurs must continuously enhance their skills and knowledge to elevate their businesses.

I have experienced that for women borrowers, accessing capital becomes a huge issue, and a certain kind of discrimination is visible. But again, it depends on the woman's outlook.

This problem is not specific to India only. Women across the globe are often faced with challenges in accessing finance, such as availing of a business loan, lowering the credit limit, and increasing the credit card limit.

The credit crunch in the MSME landscape has further complicated this issue. Women or men entrepreneurs are not able to sustain their businesses. Also, many women are venturing into startups. They have to run from pillar to post to get the credit limit sanctioned.

Choosing the right loan is equally important; it is as essential as receiving money. The pivotal factors like repayment options and loan costs will directly impact your business's bottom line. Therefore, all entrepreneurs, especially women entrepreneurs, should work with a lender who understands their financial needs and helps transform their vision for their business into a successful reality.

Do you need capital to run a **successful business**?

Yes, women fear filling out the applications; they feel it is like filling up some Ivy League application.

If you approach me, I will walk you through filling these applications with the right plan and proper funding.

However, before we go into this, let us analyze the following:

1. What type of capital do I need?
2. Which type of investor will help me reach my goals?
3. When to raise the capital, what is the right time?
4. Where to learn how to get the finance for your business?
5. Am I willing to have external control over my business?

What type of capital do I need?

Let us review the various sources of capital that are available:

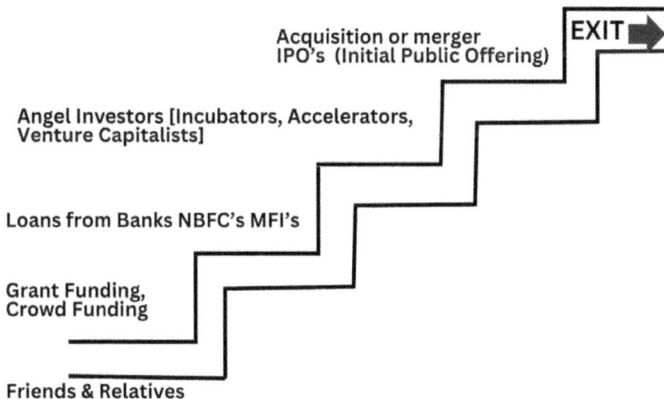

These are the different avenues women entrepreneurs can explore to secure capital and funding for their businesses, each with unique characteristics and requirements.

What is Crowdfunding?

Crowdfunding is funding a project/venture or social cause, such as medical/education/sports, or a common goal by raising donations from many individuals.

Before we explore Crowdfunding, let us distinguish it from Fundraising to avoid confusion and define Crowdfunding accurately.

Getting to the absolute basics: We called it "**Chanda**" (donation) back then, and this term is popular even now. All Inner Wheel Clubs and other small clubs are funded through the Chanda system. Mainly a group of women or men contribute money for a social cause or specific not-for-profit projects.

Therefore, seeking financial support for a cause or a charity, as mentioned earlier, is called fundraising. It reaches more audiences because, for example, the president of Inner Wheel starts a fundraising campaign for a reason and has a lot of followers/ support, and the supporters persuade their networks to garner more support.

Some people opine that fundraising is more potent than crowdfunding. However, this needs to be clarified. Let us remember that today social media tools and the internet play a vital role and create trends for crowdfunding more successfully than fundraising. Did you know that in 2015, over US$34 billion was raised using crowdfunding?

Crowdfunding originates in the West and is one of the best financing options for any social, medical, or other projects, especially those with mass appeal. For example, this may include the building of worshipping places like Mandirs and Gurudwaras. The organizers can get funding and venture by raising money from many people. Depending on their capabilities and eagerness, people can contribute any minor or substantial amount as donations. And the donors are called investors. In India, it is the most popular form of contribution, as mentioned earlier, called "Chanda," or donation.

Now, let us learn about the different types of crowdfunding:

Types of Crowdfunding

These can be broadly divided into two types: equity-based and reward-based crowdfunding. Equity-based funding is illegal in India. It is a joint effort made by people from another organization to support the cause of other people in the form of equity. It falls under the jurisdiction of SEBI and is illegal. However, it is legal in the United States. It is mentioned in the 2012 legislation that it allows a pool of small investors to come together.

Reward-based funding is also widely used for funding campaigns like supporting specific software development, promoting motion pictures, or supporting scientific research and development of inventions. People who are investing are hopeful of returns. Some popular crowdfunding sites are Kick-starter, Wishberry, Indiegogo, Ketto, Catapooolt, Fueladream, Fundable, Milaap, etc. Kickstarter is one of the first sites in India. Kickstarter and Indiegogo generally invest in a company where one can pre-buy the product.

Some crowdfunding organizations are already operational and have proven to be good options for startups. They have chosen crowdfunding routes like Fundable and Dream Wallets. Some are reward-based and are meant for creative products and services. In contrast, others act as a marketplace where entrepreneurs and investors get to interact with each other and strike deals for lending-based or social crowdfunding.

Crowdfunding platforms in India provide a straightforward and efficient way for innovators, social entrepreneurs, and startups to raise funds. They offer a user-friendly alternative to the complex fundraising methods involving bank loans, venture capital, and angel investors.

For women entrepreneurs, crowdfunding is often a quicker and more accessible way to secure capital compared to traditional sources. The key to success in crowdfunding is to create compelling videos, offer attractive packages, and leverage various sources, including friends and family, to garner support. Additionally, offering tempting rewards can incentivize backers to contribute. You can browse through the crowdfunding sites mentioned above for more information and assistance in launching your fundraising campaign.

But be careful and go through all the details. Some sites may allow you to keep the money if only your entire plan is worked out.

In the upcoming sections, we will learn more about venture capital and angel investing.

Moreover, before raising money, startups must consider the different funding stages to decide how to raise funds.

Bank loans

This is the most traditional way to take loan for small businesses. The time when I became an entrepreneur, banks were considered the priority for small business startups.

Almost all public and private banks in India provide two types of loans: working capital and term loans for plant and machinery. Business startups can avail of loan facilities from the bank on almost all kinds of products. The interest rate varies from bank to bank. It is more comfortable and easy to take a bank loan than angel investing or venture capital. The banks give the loan against collateral, such as assets or property.

How to access the bank -You can access any bank and complete all necessary paperworkwith the help of your chartered accountant. All the funding agencies require a business plan in place, along with all other details. If it is a private limited company, you must own 51% share as a woman entrepreneur. You have to be clear about who will be the authorized signatory. It is always advisable to apply for a loan from the branch where you are already banking, as you do not have to prove your credibility. Another way is to go through the references of a friend or relative.

In the 1980s, when I required a small loan to support my trading business, I secured it by leveraging my connection with a friend who worked at a bank. Later, when I needed a larger loan to establish an industrial unit and acquire working capital, I once again turned to my network, this time approaching the Oriental Bank of Commerce with the assistance of a friend associated with my husband.

However, these days, things have changed considerably. The government is coming forward to make it easy for women to raise funds for their startups. Many schemes have been introduced for the benefit of women entrepreneurs to get financial assistance/ loans with ease, and low interest rates along with a range of choices and alternatives, namely Mudra loans and Bandhan Banks.

My First Outside Investor

According to my business plan, I required a working capital of 50 lakhs. This included provisions for extending credit to customers and dealers, bill discounting, stock facilities, and other financial needs. Typically, banks would grant approximately fifty percent of the requested amount. I often wondered why they were not more optimistic and had doubts about the business plan. When the business plan projected a credit facility for 90 days, banks would calculate it for a period of 60 days. Such calculations would result in funds being tied up in outstanding credit, leading to a cash crunch for entrepreneurs. This was a common practice among banks during that time.

In the 1980s, most entrepreneurs faced a similar fate, except for those whose business models were cash-rich, such as beauty salons, education services, spas, health and wellness centers, restaurants, and more. Banks typically required entrepreneurs to provide collateral assets as a risk guarantee. During that period, the interest rates were the same for both male and female entrepreneurs, without any special benefits for women. However, some banks now offer lower interest rates to women entrepreneurs. For instance, the State Bank of India provides a 0.5% lower interest rate for loans exceeding Rs. 2 lakhs if women own at least 50% of the capital.

State Financing Corporations used to offer benefits to women entrepreneurs in terms of margin money. While male entrepreneurs typically had a margin money requirement of 25%, women entrepreneurs were only required to provide 10% as margin money.

Now, let us review the five most popular small business loans for women entrepreneurs offered by banks in India.

1. Central Bank of India: Cent Kalyani – MSME Loan Interest rate: 7.35% onwards offers business and startup loans to women entrepreneurs for new or existing businesses.

2. State Bank of India: Stree Shakti Package from SBI – Interest rate: 11.20% onwards; a business loan for women-owned businesses with no security required— competitive interest rates with 50% financing for accessories.

3. Canara Bank category includes Srinagar and Annapurna 4.a.

4. Syndicate Bank: Synd Mahila Shakti targets both new and current women entrepreneurs.

5. Bank of Baroda: Shakti Scheme: Discount of 0.25% on the interest rate on Two-Wheeler Loans. 25% waiver on processing charges for Auto loans and Mortgage Loans. 100% waiver in Processing charges for Personal Loan. 25% waiver on issuance charges of Travel/ Gift Card. The Shakti Scheme covers various sectors, like manufacturing and services. Loan for agriculture and allied activities, retail trade, and microcredit. It also offers education, housing, and enterprises in direct/indirect financial support to active women entrepreneurs. The maximum ceiling on the loans differs based on the sector. The loan is offered with no processing fee and a rebate of 0.5% on loans up to Rs. 5 lakhs.

For Women entrepreneurs' business loans, there are various Government loan schemes like Mudra Yojana, PMEGP (Prime Minister's Employment Generation Program) by KVIC, CGTMSE (CREDIT Guarantee Fund Trust for Micro and Small Enterprises), Startup India, Standup India, CGTMSE is a credit guarantee scheme by SIDBI.

You can utilize the funds for procuring raw materials, working capital, marketing, and the workforce.

The Indian Government introduced the New MSME (Medium, Small, and Micro Enterprises) definition of the 'Atma Nirbhar Bharat Abhiyan' Scheme in 2020. MSME loans are also called SME (small and medium enterprises) loans. Usually, these MSME loans are granted to small business owners, startup owners, and women entrepreneurs with subjective loan tenure.

Your 'Business Plan' based on credit rating, business profits, and revenues is what determines your final loan amount.

CGTMSE is a unique scheme introduced for MSMEs (Medium, Small, and Micro Enterprises), which has increased its scope for entrepreneurs to make it more beneficial. It covers the guarantee for entrepreneurs up to 80%. Micro and small enterprises are operated and owned by northeast estates, and women entrepreneurs have special consideration.

The enterprises eligible under this scheme are: New as well as existing MSME in the following businesses-

    a.   manufacturing activity
    b.   service activity, except Retail Trade, Educational Institutions, Self-help groups, and Training Institutions

Selected NBFCs (Non-banking Financial Companies) and MFIs (Micro Finance Institutions) also offer small business loans, which you can avail for your startup based on your requirements. You can apply for the loan even if you do not have a credit score or financial history.

If you are new to borrowing, getting loans from private or public sector banks may become challenging as they may ask for your financial history or credit score. Compared to PSU (Public Sector Undertaking) banks, the interest rates offered by NBFCS and MFIs are comparatively higher.

Peer-to-Peer Lending

RBI regulates peer-to-peer lending institutions. It is a type of lending where no intermediaries are involved in the whole process. Lenders lend money to borrowers at a higher interest rate on their investments. The borrowers can operate on the reward-based money model at their disposal to invest in their startup. Compared to banks, NBFCs, and MFIs, peer-to-peer lending is known for bettering lenders and borrowers.

Ms. Iti Rawat, Founder and Director at Think Hall Academy

She is the Founder and Director of Thinkhall Training and Consultancy and the Founder of the WEFT (Women Entrepreneurs Foundation). She has successfully established and managed a Training and Consulting firm, which has received recognition as a Top 5 Startup in Diversity Human Resource Services and Consultants. In addition, she leads a not-for-profit organization dedicated to supporting women entrepreneurs in India. She is also the creator of the RED DOT INITIATIVE, a program that has assisted over 250 domestic violence survivors. Her company, Thinkhall, was honored as Business in Focus 2021 by Business Connect Magazine and was incubated by NSRCEL, IIM Bangalore, and accelerated by ISB, Mohali.

When you started as CEO of Think Hall and Founder of Red Dot, you must have stepped away from day-to-day work. How does that happen?

I worked with retail companies in the past. I was working with Arvin, then I moved to Nike, and then I worked with Apple, my last job.

I have been in retail for the past 20 years. We have been doing training and development in retail for the past seven years. We have opened the market for other industries. We have acquired one person from the Automobile industry, one from FMPG, and one from FMCD. So we are accepting clients from different sectors. My husband is associated with Think Hall, but it is primarily managed by me, only like a single women's army.

We started WEFT. It is for women entrepreneurs. It is not for profit. We were supporting women entrepreneurs with conferences and videos. We highlighted the issue of domestic violence with the Red Dot initiative, and it became pretty successful.

We are working on the ideas of women farmers. We are working on making more entrepreneurs. A project started in Chennai where we collaborated with a tea company and trained women, then facilitated them by opening a tea stall.

We are doing Skill Development through Think Hall. It is online content. One can complete a one-year course and can go onward like that. It is endless. Previously we were doing it on a system-wise model, but now we are doing it on a subscription model, like one subscription for Hindi and another for English, and in the future, we will try to make it in other languages, as well.

How did your first company get finances?

We funded it from our savings. We are currently seeking a bank loan for Think Hall due to the impact of the COVID-19 pandemic, which has caused delays in payments. We need the loan to cover employee salaries. I initially approached Lending Kart, but their interest rates were quite high.

I also visited SBI (State Bank of India) and SIDBI (Small Industries Development Bank of India). SIDBI informed me that since my business is service-based, they would not provide a loan.

In the case of SBI, I had the opportunity to meet an accommodating and proactive individual. I am hopeful that my loan will be sanctioned through SBI.

What was your first round of Angel investment?

I am approaching Angel Investors interested in the Skill Development area. I am in touch with Matt company, Ken Capital, One Angel, also Mr. Saroj Patro. I am in touch with many of them and trying to find a way. As far as their stakes are concerned, different people will be asking for other stakes. But I am very clear about what I have to give. I am proposing 2 crores to 10 crores and trying to give 10-15% of it. They will agree, and it is a good deal.

During a meeting with an angel investor alongside Gaurav, I noticed that the investor consistently directed his attention towards Gaurav, even when I was responding to his questions. This made me uncomfortable, as it felt like I was being ignored. The investor then posed a question that further spotlighted the biases I was facing. He asked, "Why are you involved in multiple things? If you manage the business, who will take care of the kids?" This experience served as a stark reminder of the prevalent biases in the entrepreneurial world.

The best investors typically inquire about your company's growth, your goals, your vision, how much funding you require, and your plans for utilizing the funds. However, there are instances when investors ask unusual questions, such as inquiring about your hobbies and other non-professional topics.

Do you have other tips about Angel Investing?

Believe in yourself and your vision. Go out with a positive attitude without considering what the investor feels about you or your proposal. Most investors are ready to fund your business if you have a vital project and a positive attitude.

Angel Investor

The researchers say that in almost all major countries like America, Canada, Russia, China; angel investing started in the year 2000 onwards. There were few, less than 50, Angel Investors in the Indian Startup Ecosystem in the early 2000s. However, today it has grown to a massive number.

After bank loans, family, and friends, we come to the next stop of Angel Investors. Angel investors are those individuals who have the financial capabilities and freedom to invest in a venture along with strategic insights for startup growth and expansion, and it seems profitable to them. In this case, the investor should be knowledgeable and expert. Angel Investing is a common way between a loan from a bank or family and friends for venture capital to create a stage where the critical performance indicators attract more investments.

To begin with, you can research online who funded your competitors. Angel Investors are those people who have extra disposable income and are ready to invest in others' businesses on some profit-sharing or shareholding basis. You can find many angel investors through your product search or online sources where you can get lost. So, the best way to approach an Angel Investor is through mutual contact. Professional Angel Investors will like to do the due diligence on your portfolio and work in a specific sector they follow. You will find Angel Investors in all major cities of India, like Mumbai, Delhi, Hyderabad, Chennai, and many more. You may enter the name of the town followed by the Angel Investor as the keywords. You can get your project running within three to five months.

As per the report of 2018, Indian startups raised around $173 million in **Pre-Series A and Angel rounds.** The hands-on experience, the access to a vast network, and the extensive resources make Angel Investors invaluable to startups.

These investments by Angel Investors are more at risk than financial institutions. Such investors are high-net-worth individuals seeking a higher return rate than traditional investments. They are mentors and guides who may or may not get involved in the day-to-day management of the business, depending on their share and terms. Also, they bring sufficient relevant assets to the partnership regarding expertise and knowledge.

It is daunting for first-time entrepreneurs to raise capital for their businesses. Almost all Angel Investors have a list of checkboxes before they take an interest in your project or give guidance and time to your startup. These checkboxes need to be filled.

A known fact is that 90% of startups fail within five years of their operations in India. Therefore, a successful approach for young startups would be to tie up with Angel Investors at the early start stage. These Angel Investors are seasoned entrepreneurs. They have all the knowledge, experience, understanding, and proper mindset to help a budding entrepreneur. Apart from providing capital, these angels also offer mentorship and help to connect to the right people in the industry. They can play a significant role in delivering growth opportunities.

At least 25 or more Angel Investors have already taken initiatives. You can find them in all cities or close to your place. I spoke to a few entrepreneurs/startups and found that women still need help to secure funding from Angel investors. The biggest hurdle is the mindset which men generally find hard to change.

Venture Capital

Venture Capitalists are those who make very high investments. After the Angel Investor, venture capital is the right source of funding. It could be a laborious task to gather venture capital. To graduate from a small to a large company, one should start from a bank or seed capital, move to an angel investor, and then approach a venture capitalist.

Venture capital is the money provided by professionals who invest in a young, rapidly growing company with the potential to develop immensely. It is also an essential source of equity for startup companies.

Venture capital is the backbone of the financial market today. Venture capital is the most challenging kind of money for every entrepreneur; it started in India in a big way, regardless of gender. The venture capitalist provides cash to the entrepreneurs and extends guidance and expert support in achieving a viable business venture. It is becoming prevalent in India. The success of information and technology in India has proven a tremendously promising future for the knowledge-based industry. The IT sector's recent economic slowdown has provided venture capitalists a chance and has opened opportunities for other sectors, like the manufacturing and service industry, education, and many more. Venture capital is an essential source of equity for startup companies. Now there are great companies with the potential to develop into significant economic contributors.

Indian companies attracted around 10 billion US dollars in venture capital investments in 2020. It was slightly minor as compared to the record-breaking year 2019. As the number of deals increased, it is still the country's second-highest value of VC investments.

The investment trend continues as the value of VC investments remains high despite the implications of the coronavirus (COVID-19) pandemic. Emerging sectors like Fintech and Software as a Service (SaaS) have influenced large deals.

A recent study shows that The National Venture Capital Association has found that only 17 percent of Venture Capitalists in America plan to increase their investment in the US over the next three years. These investors are more interested in investing in India and Asian countries for a better return on investment.

Venture capitalists can invest anywhere from Rs.100,000, called seed capital, at the early investment stage and go up to billions, covering all manufacturing, development, and marketing expenses.

The company can seek additional capital if the business has yet to yield any profit and expand its line of products, operations, inventories, and technology; once the company has matured, bridge financing allows it to go public. The investors and shareholders can restructure positions, and their agreement can be exited (an exit strategy).

I had an informal talk with a venture capitalist, and he expressed that they get around 500 pitches every year from startup founders who want Venture Partners to invest in their business, and only 1% gets converted and funded.

The specific requirements can vary based on the type of business and the location. I suggest consulting professionals and the relevant government authorities to ensure accurate and timely completion of applications. Additionally, the government of India has been actively promoting digital initiatives, so checking out online platforms for application submissions can often streamline the process.

Is Your Company Scalable?

Determining whether your company is scalable requires a comprehensive evaluation of various factors.

1. ***Assess your business model***: Examine your current business model to understand if it has the potential for growth and expansion. Consider if your product or service can be easily replicated or delivered to a larger customer base without significant constraints.

2. ***Market size and demand***: Evaluate the size of your target market and the potential demand for your product

or service. A scalable business typically operates in a large and growing market with a substantial customer base.

3. **Revenue streams**: Analyze your revenue streams to determine if they have the potential to scale. Assess whether your business can generate increased revenue without proportionate increases in costs. Look for opportunities to diversify your revenue streams and explore new markets.

4. **Operational efficiency**: Examine your business operations and processes to identify opportunities for efficiency and scalability. Streamline workflows, automate tasks where possible, and optimize your resources to handle increasing demand without compromising quality.

5. **Scalable infrastructure**: Evaluate your infrastructure, including technology systems, production capacity, and distribution channels. Ensure that your infrastructure can support rapid growth and easily adapt to increased demand.

6. **Human resources and talent**: Consider if your organization has the capacity to scale. Assess your team's capabilities, skills, and scalability potential. Determine if you have the right talent in place and if you can attract and retain additional skilled employees as your business grows.

7. **Financial analysis**: Conduct a thorough financial analysis to assess the financial feasibility of scaling your business. Evaluate your revenue projections, cost structures, profitability, and funding requirements. Determine if scaling will result in sustainable growth and positive cash flow.

8. **Scalability roadblocks**: Identify any potential roadblocks or challenges that may hinder your business's scalability. Assess factors such as regulatory constraints, competition, supply chain limitations, or technological barriers. Develop strategies to mitigate these obstacles.

9. **Testing and validation**: Validate your business scalability assumptions through testing and piloting.

Conduct market tests, launch pilot projects, or explore expansion into new regions to validate the scalability potential of your business model.

10. ***Continuous monitoring and adjustment***: Scalability is an ongoing process. Continuously monitor your business's performance, gather feedback, and adapt your strategies as needed. Stay agile and responsive to market dynamics and customer demands. Scalability is not a guarantee of success but an indication of your business's potential to grow rapidly and sustainably. Regularly reassess and refine your strategies to maximize your chances of successfully scaling your company.

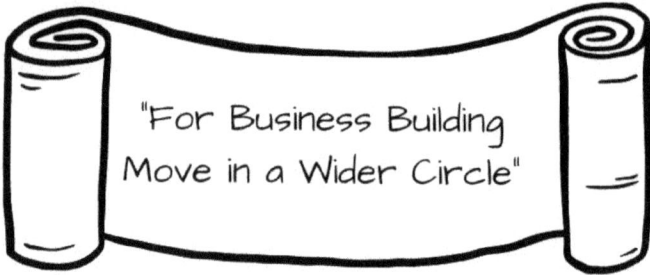

"For Business Building Move in a Wider Circle"

How do you choose to meet a VC (venture capitalist)?

The vital factor is that they prefer to meet people recommended by friends, VCs, and other founders. CEOs, angel investors. It is easy for high-quality connections to introduce the people who can meet the VCs.

So, when looking for an investor, start with your network.

Do Your Research

- LinkedIn is the best source if you are looking for a second or third-degree connection working with VC firms.
- Any entrepreneur who can introduce you to anyone.
- Go to Networking events and tech-up meets.

- Search for portfolio pages of the sites of VCs to see whom they have invested with, meet those CEOs, and invite them for a coffee. If it goes well, ask for an introduction.
- Use Twitter and LinkedIn to see your target whom VCs are interacting with and either make or find a connection with them.

So, having learned about how we can approach VCs, you can think of going for venture capital if you meet the following criteria:

1. Your company envisages a market worth Rs. I billion.
2. You have an exit plan in place, take your Company Public within 5 to 7 years, and generate a high return.
3. Yours is a fast-growing company with doubled revenues over the years.
4. You want to increase the value of your company by increasing your staff, spending more on marketing, and may even forget profitability for a certain period.
5. A new investor on your board can determine that you are not the right person to lead a company at some point. In this case, you will retain the ownership but will not be at the helm of affairs.
6. You are ready to work with VC. It might call for changing your old staff, reducing your cost of goods, and introducing a new strategic partnership.

As VCs are your partners who will bring good contacts and high resources, you can revamp your staff, marketing, operations, and product development with the infusion of their money. It's good for your business. But remember, VCs generally get 2 or 3 seats on the board and 20 to 30 percent equity (ownership) of the company.

Venture capital is highly demanding, and there is pressure on scaling up and growing aggressively. You must continuously monitor the company and its positioning to know when to exit. Review regularly if your calculations and projections are on track or not. Reviewing can help you evaluate whether to sell the company to some prominent investor, strategic partner, or public offering.

However, venture capital may not be an option if you want to build a business for your family to run.

You can take money from the bank, family, or friends or hire a mediating company to get the loan for you at a cost. Sometimes, these specialists ask for retainers' money, which is a handsome amount plus a 5 percent to 7 percent commission. I suggest you borrow the money from family, friends, or advisors.

Which Type of Investor will Help Me Reach My Goals?

It would be best if you decided based on your urgency and ease. Every capital has a different requirement and period. Smaller loans can take from 1 month to three months. Banks can take three months to five months to go through the process and come to a conclusion.

Raising money through an Angel Investor is more of a sprint that will retake 3 to 4 months from your pitch, whereas Venture Capital is like a marathon.

Who decides what your company's worth is?

The company's valuation will show how much ownership you have after the investment is made. The first round of funding should preferably comprise family and friends. It all depends on how you project yourself, showing a strong and credible projection and comparing your future predictions to a successful business in your space.

- Business valuation determines the economic value of a business or business unit.
- Funders can use business valuation to determine a business's fair value for various reasons, including sale value, establishing partner ownership, taxation, and divorce proceedings.
- Several methods of valuing a business exist, such as its market cap, earnings multipliers, or book value.

Company valuation, also known as business valuation, is the process of assessing the total economic value of a business and its assets. During this process, all aspects of a company are evaluated to determine the current worth of an organization or department. The valuation process occurs for various reasons, such as deciding sale value and tax reporting.

Who is Investing money?

Investors will want to see information that indicates the business's current financial status. Usually, they will expect to see recent reports such as a profit and loss statement, a balance sheet, and a cash flow statement. Angel Investor or Venture Capital would like to see the future projections.

The source of investment can vary depending on the stage of your business and your specific circumstances. Both angel investors and venture capital firms can be potential sources of investment for scaling your company.

Angel investors are typically high-net-worth individuals who invest their funds in early-stage or startup companies. They often provide capital in exchange for equity ownership in the company. Angel investors can offer financial support, mentorship, industry expertise, and valuable connections. They are more inclined to invest in businesses during their initial stages when the risk is higher, but the potential for significant returns is also present.

Venture capital firms are investment firms that pool funds from various sources, such as institutional investors, high-net-worth individuals, and corporations. They invest in startups and early-stage companies with high growth potential. VC firms typically invest more significant sums than individual angel investors, often providing additional support such as strategic guidance, industry networks, and operational expertise. Venture capital investments usually happen in exchange for equity or convertible debt.

The choice between angel investors and venture capital depends on several factors, including the stage of your business, funding needs, industry, growth potential, and the investors' preferences. Early-stage startups often rely on angel investors for initial funding to develop their products or services and gain traction. As the company progresses and demonstrates growth potential, venture capital firms may become more interested in investing expansive amounts to help scale the business.

Please note that these are not the only sources of investment.

Other options include crowdfunding, grants, loans, strategic partnerships, and government programs, which may vary depending on your location and industry. Dr. Shobha Dhawan does not believe in going to an angel or venture for funding. She is confident about banking support which is comparatively more straightforward and accessible.

When seeking investment, thoroughly research and understand potential investors' specific requirements, expectations, and investment criteria. Tailor your approach and pitch to align with their investment focus and expertise.

Engage with professional networks, attend industry events, and seek advice from experienced entrepreneurs or advisors who can guide you through the investment process and help you connect with suitable investors.

Amitabh Sinha, Co-founder and Chief Strategy Officer, meetingsandoffices.com | Chairman, Growth Kinetics | Code Breaker, Dcyphr | Founder of SMARTup Conclave

Amitabh Sinha is a serial entrepreneur, startup evangelist, advisor, mentor, ecosystem builder, and facilitator active in the startup domain since 1999.

I would like to know what you are doing now and what you have done in the past. When you think of successful women entrepreneurs what comes to your mind?

I have a brief profile about myself written by me. I will be sharing with you. The biggest difference between men and women is that women can multitask. They are nurturers by nature, but also understand the value of risk as a tool of growth. While most men will focus on management of risk, more women will perceive risk as opportunity. They take more risk in comparison to men.

When is the right time to raise venture capital?

There is always a right time. You could raise money on the earlier level. You could put your concept on PowerPoint presentation or on a piece of paper and if you are able to convenience your capitalist you will get the funds. In India unfortunately that does not happen. The biggest problem is of understanding. Most people think that if our business is making profit it is fundable, others think just any business is fundable. Neither is true. A fundable business is one that has the potential to generate multiples of valuation and can do so quickly.

What do you think women entrepreneurs should do differently to secure venture capital?

Nothing at all. That is not needed. I know that there are a few segments in venture capital who think women don't do good business and all but frankly that segment is shrinking fairly rapidly. In fact far more people recognize the fact that women are so well capable of doing business at least as well as men. Proof that women can treat their stake holders very well when it comes to creating wealth, is out there in abundance. So, I don't think that women need to do anything differently. They should not go with a begging bowl in hand and with an attitude that the person who is going to invest in your business is going to do you a favor, because the investors are taking calculated risks, that all. If the business produces multiples on equity, investors make money. It's a fairly balanced relationship.

Do you think men are any different in that respect i.e. they are doing anything differently that women are not doing?

No not at all. Sometimes men have their edges because of the networks that exists but I don't think there is something differently done by them.

Is there any point where fund raising becomes very important?

Yes, there is always a point in the kind of business that we are talking about, that is a fundable business, where relying on your internal resource generation will not allow you to capitalize. That is the time you must raise money. There is nothing more important than growth of the business in optimal time and circumstances.

I have heard that there are 3 or 4 women who have started Angel investing groups.

Globally, yes, but in India, Amisha from Mydala has started it. I am not so sure, but yes percentage of women in Angel Investing in India is gradually increasing.

If you have clarity about the right time:

1. **You can scale more quickly.**
2. **You gain credibility.**
3. **You can tap resources beyond just money.**
4. **You receive assistance with risk and strategic direction.**
5. **You can enjoy generous funding terms.**

My approach to identifying entrepreneurship skills is to examine venture-capital-backed serial entrepreneurs' performance.

Are successful entrepreneurs more skilled and likely to succeed in their next venture than first-time entrepreneurs?

The ratio is 30% success compared to first-time entrepreneurs, with an 18% success rate. The ones who have failed earlier have a 20% success rate. So, the answer is yes. This persistent performance is attributed to their skills. They say it may be better to be lucky than brilliant, but the evidence proves that being smart has value too.

Skill is an essential component of entrepreneurship. Suppliers of capital are not just efficient risk bearers in the entrepreneurial process, but they have the capabilities to identify skilled entrepreneurs and help them build their businesses.

How long should you plan to raise capital for your startup?

This is a big question that entrepreneurs must reflect on. Successful entrepreneurs who raised pre-seed and seed rounds must have worked to keep the show going and, more precisely, in the timely fundraising follow-up.

Source: How long is too long? Alejandro Cremades, the author of The Art of Startup Fundraising and Serial Entrepreneur

Raising Pre-Seed Money

The most challenging part is to get startup capital. If you are a serial entrepreneur, it may be easier because you have had a successful exit or two and have a network of viable investors eager to fund. But only some entrepreneurs are in this bucket. The most critical factor is speed.

As we know, ideas are valuable, and we must work on them and hit the market speedily. There have been rivals to Uber, too, in raising millions of dollars. Many founders need help in this fundraising process and take a shorter way to reach somewhere.

However, this does not mean that you lose hope and give up quickly.

It may take time if you have no network or are new in the business. You may have to file many numbers before you get a cheque. But if you are doing the right things, you can achieve this in lessthan 12 months. Get all your ducks in a row, get the cash, and get started.

If your requirement is small, focus on getting enough to reach the next stage.

Multiple Fundraising Rounds

Startups are raising money every year. The Entrepreneurs who can master the art of storytelling with a pitch deck of no more than 15 slides are the best fundraisers. For a winning deck, refer to the template created by *Silicon Valley legend Peter Thiel*. He was the first angel investor on Facebook with $500k, which got converted into $1 billion cash. Also, check a commentary on a pitch deck that has raised over $400M from an Uber competitor.

You are raising money to move to the next milestone. At every next level, you are proving your worth and attracting investors.

On average, this takes 12 to 18 months to seek loan approval. During this period, you may set up yourself by borrowing money from friends and family. Do more research, survive a year, and prepare your prototype. Then start fundraising for bigger sums. After reaching series B and C rounds, you may be working to bring new capital in 15 to 20 months.

You may have to anticipate the time from raising to getting money in the bank.

The Fundraising Process in Six Simple Steps:

1. Gather your data on achievements and forecast your financial needs
2. Prepare your pitch deck
3. Start reaching out to potential investors with your ask
4. Attend investor meetings
5. Field term sheets and proposals
6. Survive the due diligence process

It takes time to coordinate. It could take about months in the due diligence process alone. The investor could work on and investigate your statements versus your business status.

Most people do not share this with you; the investors consider your business's fundable value against their criteria. So, keep the pitch aligned with the perspective that the investors should be nurturing.

The Startup Fundraising

Fundraising can be time-consuming. Therefore, the fundraisers must keep their schedules in place and be as effective as possible during fundraising. Be in contact with potential investors every single day.

The Biggest Factors Impacting Timing in Fundraising

1. The time of year you are raising.
2. The strength and depth of your data.
3. The quality and effectiveness of your pitch deck.
4. Your pitch presentation and performance in investor meetings.
5. The strength of your relationship with investors.
6. How complicated is due diligence?
7. How fast does the lead investor in each round move?
8. How organized are your accounting records?
9. Your location.
10. Availability of Capital, market trends, and appetite investments for startups.

What if it Takes Too Long to Raise Capital?

While the processing is happening, for you, it's time to prepare and learn about best practices and strategies. Consult a panel of experts to review your pitch deck and business idea, which may help connect you to an investor interested in funding your venture.

Evaluate the time it takes to raise capital for a startup. Plan at least six months to open and take an exit. It is a marathon in comparison, but there are ways to speed up the process. Constant relationship-building with current and future investors is essential.

Where to learn how to get the finance for your business?

Getting your business loan is complicated, but if you carefully prepare all your documents, your chances for approval are bright.

You must provide the banker with a well-researched document and a clear business plan. This will urge them to consider your proposal; it will convey that you have the vision and neck of everything it takes to succeed in business.

You should explain how you will reap profit and pay back their loans.

The following four keys are essential to getting business loans:

1. Show your confidence that you have the skills to manage your business.
2. Research well to make a good business plan.
3. Invest in your own company.
4. Know your personal credit history.

Now, if you want to reach venture capitalists, do a little research to find out about their backgrounds, if it suits your requirements, and if they accept your space. The investor's background check is crucial. The best practice is to have a friendly introduction. But if you cannot find a direct connection, consider the 4 Ps: your product, passion, people, and praise.

I have the following advice for entrepreneurs; take care of what to say and whatnot:

1. VCs are greatly bombarded with meeting letters. Therefore, it is always good to have an introduction letter so that they know your background and it is possible to come to the top.
2. Research the VCs if they are relevant to your business idea.
3. Reach out to the VC in a way that makes it easy for him to respond to your approach.
4. Be specific about why you are approaching that VC and what you want to accomplish. Should you send an email or leave a message? Give the VC enough information

about your requirement to determine whether it is of interest to him.

5. Provide the VC with enough information during the initial approach to allow him to analyze if you and your opportunity are interesting.

6. Successful fundraisings are usually small steps rather than one giant step. You have to provide all the relevant information to the VC so that one gets interested and responds. Like an expression of interest, you must submit all the details, and then you can proceed with the fundraising dance.

7. Follow through when you make your outreach, and be gently persistent.

8. Do not try to be informed as a prelude to your "ask."

9. Only create a lot of hype if you can back it up. Do not create a false sense of urgency and do not do name drop.

Consider the 4 Ps: your product, passion, people, and praise.

The VCs typically take from 12 months to 18 months to decide on your funding after complete documentation, calculation, and finally, how you pitch. Fine-tuning your business pitch creates a final impression or confidence in VCs based on what they decide in your favor. You need to know how VCs work. The in-depth knowledge about VC's work will help you prepare your business plan, deck, and pitch, along with the time of processing your application. You can wait and arrange your finances in that gap created by the application process and VC's outcome. An investor analyzes all the facts and figures of a potential investment. It can include an investigation of financial records and a measure of possible ROI (Rate of Interest). VCs undoubtedly conduct due diligence.

Vigorously prepare yourself. After researching how venture capitalists work and behave, your preparation has to be three times more than your current preparation.

- You can watch videos on how to pitch on YouTube.
- Enjoy and deeply understand the episodes of SHARK TANK, a popular TV serial.

- Discuss your approach with your CEO, network friends, take some classes, and should learn to understand the language of VCs.
- Do not be fake, be yourself. If you are labeled 'more like a man' or bossy, do not bother about it.

Male VCs may ignore you or say inappropriate things; I suggest you do not get hung up about it; focus on genuine connections and people ready to help and support you. I recommend a book: *Be Smarter Than Your Lawyer and Venture Capitalist*, by Brad Feld and Jason Mendelson.

Compellingly tell your story. Feel as inspired as when you started your business. Practice pitching to investors who will never find you—practice by pitching to friends and colleagues."

Am I willing to have external control over my business?

The typical standard observed in fundraising by VC is 2 percent of the fund size and 20 percent of any liquidation that might happen. So, in any case, even if they fail to get any returns during the early stage of funding, they get up to 10 percent to 20 percent equity share from the company's founder as a general rule.

Much of it depends on the relationship between the founder and the investors, the stage of the company, its prospects, and the amount invested; the VCs will take from 25% to 50% of the company's ownership.

VC brings funds, management expertise, industry connections, and mentorship support. It is based on the High-Risk High-Return formula, as the research says. "Venture capitalists follow the Pareto principle – 80 percent of the wins come from 20 percent of the deals."

With India becoming a viable playing field for venture capitalists and entrepreneurs alike, starting a business and securing venture capital - a type of private equity provided to startup companies with high-growth potential - are becoming less tedious and frustrating processes. Through equity financing or stock issuing, entrepreneurs do not have to worry about making monthly debt payments to banks; instead, they share part ownership of their company in exchange for capital.

You should ensure that interest is aligned with your shareholder, aiming to make thethe company as profitable as possible to create a win-win situation for both. If someone can do better than me, I will gladly hand over to them and move to a different role to ensure the company achieves new heights.

Raising funds timely is very important. However, it can only happen after you decide in January that you need money in March to meet your more critical requirements. Therefore, chalk out a plan if you want to grow. Your vision should be clear and well-planned., Create a network of angel investors and venture capitalists, and ensure your documents, marketing, and team are in place.. At the same time, be prepared for your plans.

Starting with family and friends, moving to angel investors and venture capital; are the three types of investments for your growth. It is not an occasional way of fund receiving but a continual process of evolution from small to large. It opens the way forward for the continuous development of the company.

Ms. Padmaja Ruparel, Co-founder, Indian Angel Network (IAN)

Padmaja Ruparel is nationally recognized as a key player in the Indian entrepreneurial ecosystem and has helped co-found several relevant institutions, besides being an active angel investor herself. Her operating experience spans large corporations, M&A, and startups/ early-stage companies.

She has been awarded as one of the 'Top 50 Most Powerful Women in Business' by Fortune India for 4 years, is listed in Forbes India's W-Power Trailblazers and "30 Most Powerful Women in India" by Business Today for 3 years consecutively. The Women's Economic Forum felicitated her with its "Women of the Decade in Investment Banking" award. She is the Co-Founder of Indian Angel Network (IAN), India's first and now possibly one of the world's largest group of business angels, comprising the who's who of successful entrepreneurs and dynamic CEOs from India and overseas. She built IAN from inception, making it within 15 years a unique institution globally, with close to 500 investors across 10 countries and a portfolio of ~200 companies in 7 countries, spanning 17 sectors.

What type of projects are most suitable for funding?

I am responding from the perspective of an angel investor or a VC perspective.

Before I respond, it is critical to understand a few points about the model of investing. They invest in startups or early-stage companies when debt financing is not available to these companies as they do not have a "history" e.g. they will not have financials for the past three years, will be thinking of past data, etc. which typically banks need before approving debt. Hence, while banks look at the history of the company, angel and VC investors look at the future of companies, i.e., projections and probability of achieving these. Hence, these investors invest by buying shares of the company. Now their model or returns is based on an increase in share price, i.e., they buy shares at, say, Rs 200/share and look to sell them at a much higher price. For share price to increase, it is imperative for companies to grow both their top line/revenues as well as their bottom line/profits.

Therefore, for the top line to grow, there needs to be a large customer base that is growing. Hence, these investors look for companies targeting a large and growing market. Further, for a large customer base to buy, the product needs to be a "need to have" and not "nice to have": an inbuilt compulsion to buy and ideally buy repeatedly.

For a startup to even get going and build a business, its product needs to be differentiated. It cannot be manufacturing/selling a product that a large company is already into. It will not be able to compete and will be dead even before it learns to live. Hence, a strong moat is essential.

All of this is good, but unless the company has a "kickass" founder/s, there is very little probability of survival. He/she not only needs to understand the space, customer needs and strategy of the company, but he also needs to be a leader. As the company grows, he will need to build a team and retain them. His/her passion, focus and energy are instrumental.

Do you follow any specific level of investment?

I invest in seed and early-stage companies. Seed-stage is typically the initial phase of a startup's life cycle. At this point, the entrepreneur or founding team has an idea or concept for a product or service, but they may not have a fully developed business model or a working prototype. Seed-stage companies often require capital to conduct market research, build a minimum viable product (MVP), and validate their business idea. Investors who focus on the seed stage are willing to take higher risks in exchange for the potential of high returns.

Early-stage refers to the next phase in a startup's development. At this point, the company has likely progressed beyond the concept stage and has a functional product or service. Early-stage startups may have some initial customers or users and are in the process of refining their products, scaling their operations, and seeking further market validation. Investors who target early-stage companies are looking to support businesses that have moved past the riskiest stage but are not yet fully established.

What is the relationship between being good at managing a company and being good in fundraising?

Both these aspects are central for a founder, but effective cash flow management is of paramount importance. As the better revenues, collections and expenses are managed, the lesser the need for raising capital and the ensuing need for dilution. So a sharp eye on cash flows prevents quick fund raise and dilution. In the same breadth, when the company needs to raise, it must, as the business should not come to a standstill or die. Hence, fundraising is part of managing a company.

Why in the fundraising game women are not as comfortable as me?

This is an excellent question. Many women struggle with a lack of confidence and conviction in their abilities, and I believe this is the most rugged hurdle. For example, women often hesitate to discuss financial numbers. However, the reality is that they often possess a solid understanding of these figures because numbers are a direct reflection of the business. What investors truly need is a comprehensive understanding of the business, its forward strategy, potential risks, mitigation strategies, and the key individuals behind the business. Any founder, regardless of gender, can provide this essential information!

We look to men in our lives (professional or personal) if not for guidance, for endorsement of our thinking.

If you look closely, where the man has been the strength behind the woman (without really being part of their professional life), women have not only raised funding but done much more.

It is important to change the phrase "behind every successful man there is a woman" to "behind every successful person there is a partner".

Do you think women entrepreneurs should do differently to secure venture capital?

Women are shy and hesitate to speak about their achievements. When an introduction is given around the table, men are incredibly proud of their achievements.

In my personal experience, women are more likely to come to us with a well-defined product that seems painfully final, with no room to pivot. They are honest and count every single thing that can go wrong. On the other hand, their male counterparts tend to focus on the big shiny picture, which sometimes only exists on slides.

I believe I have responded to this in my response to the 4th question.

Key Takeaways

- ✤ Adequate funding is the lifeline for SME business success.
- ✤ Be aware of day-to-day operational expenses, payroll, overheads, and timely vendor payments.
- ✤ Write down unique financial needs for each project.
- ✤ Financially knowledgeable women make independent decisions and contribute effectively to various fields.
- ✤ Establish open and honest communication with debtors and creditors for negotiation.
- ✤ Assess the scalability of revenue streams, ensuring increased revenue without proportionate cost increases.
- ✤ Check the money making point in your business and how predictable it is ?Question and write what you expect to achieve by raising capital.
- ✤ Your pitch must stand out to capture investor attention.
- ✤ Thoroughly prepare for fundraising with three times the usual effort.
- ✤ Handle challenges with grace; focus on genuine connections and supportive individuals.

CHAPTER 6

Networking: Become the Power Connector

"Your network is your net worth."

– Tim Sanders

On November 1, 2017, Barack Obama hosted the inaugural Obama Foundation Summit in his hometown in Chicago. He delivered a speech conveying his inspiration behind the Obama Foundation, stating that he wanted to create "a hub, a venue, a place, a network" for young people of all backgrounds, where they would meet and learn from each other.

He emphasized creating and rearing a relationship and connecting with people who do not look like you, live in different places, and are taking the bull of challenges by the horns. The other person should have a strong point of view and disagree, but not be disagreeable. He intends to offer a platform for exchanging ideas because ideas are the currency of this era. His mission is to cultivate future leaders, inspire and empower people to change the world.

So, do not bother about religion, gender, and race, be rooted in your experience, and do not hesitate to share with others. Share the joy of your small success, which can be a big hit.

When you are young, people recognize you for your competence. However, when you cross forty or fifty years, what works is your networking. We are very social. Generally, we think of Networking in terms of being social. However, it has a much broader spectrum. In India, you are known as a socialite when you are seen all over at conferences, seminars, events, talk shows, dinner parties. Interestingly, good networking starts with introspection. With limited time and resources, you must be very clear about how networking can be more rewarding.

Sometimes, it is a selfish, unpleasant task involving trading favors with strangers.

We may feel it is unethical, but we must challenge our leadership roles and think to rethink them as leaders do. This transition into a leadership role is essential for establishing a personal connection.

Through networking, you can create personal contact, get feedback and support, insight, and become resourceful. Most importantly, networking helps aspiring leaders accept change.

Regardless of your motivations, networking is generally most effective (and more rewarding) when you try to share your skills and experiences as others share theirs. It is a two-way process.

For some, the focus could be primarily professional; for others, entirely social. Some seek support, while others look for self-improvement opportunities.

The word "work" has a reasoned place in the term Networking. This work means you have to WORK at it. However, when done with unfaltering intention and effort, you will find the personal and professional rewards are worthwhile.

The reason you are actively participating in various events and gatherings is to expand your network and establish more connections intentionally. You have a clear understanding of the noteworthiness of these activities for both your business and personal development. Ibarra and Hunter (2007) conducted a study on networking, as mentioned in the *Harvard Business Review*, and they suggest concentrating on cultivating three specific types of networks. In contrast, you define separate but interconnected forms of networking within three distinct categories.

- Personal
- Operational
- Strategic

Personal Network

Personal networking involves connecting with friends and acquaintances who may not be directly associated with your professional work or organization, but are willing to provide personal support and assistance in your personal growth. This type of networking often occurs through participation in alumni groups, clubs, professional associations, and communities related to personal interests, such as Inner Wheel or Rotary clubs.

To effectively build your personal network, consider these essential steps:

- Join alumni groups, professional associations, and personal interest communities.
- Develop your professional skills through training, coaching, or mentoring.
- Share referrals and valuable external information with your network.

Personal networking primarily occurs with individuals outside of your organization, and it involves your efforts to identify personal growth opportunities among your contacts. This network consists of your circle of casual acquaintances, including those you may meet in social clubs, music clubs, drama clubs, book reading clubs, local social clubs, as well as friends and relatives. The relevance of these connections is often based on your discretion and individual preferences.

Operational Network

Your support system should consist of people who can help you accomplish your assigned, routine tasks. It is identifying individuals who can block or support a project.

You get your work done efficiently under your guidance and knowledge. You should identify individuals who are knowledgeable and can support your project.

Strategic Network

Plan and identify people who can help you determine how your role and contribution fit into the overall picture of people outside your immediate control. Identify lateral and vertical relationships with other functional and business unit managers.

We should figure out future priorities and challenges. Most personal networks are a large group of friends, it is like my friends are likely to be friends with one another as well. In addition, if those friends are directly your friends and you know them through a mutual acquaintance, there are huge chances that your experiences and perspectives echo within your group.

Knowing your Business and Goals

Various internal and external contacts are available for relevant opportunities to attend different events and business platforms. You may join some business associations like the Federation of Indian Women Entrepreneurs (FIWE) and Women Chamber of Commerce (WICCI), and business associations like FICCI Ladies Organization, Confederation of Indian Industries (CII), (ASSOCHAM) or The Indus Entrepreneurs (TIE).

2007- Award for Outstanding Work and Excellence
for Empowerment and Social Service as Rotarian

159

These associations are bankable platforms as they endow knowledge and information on business policies. Besides, if you can use these platforms smartly to associate yourself with relevant people, you can string along with pertinent people to your work, like bankers, experts, lawyers, judges, and other senior officials from the government. These connections help you riddle out the problems you may face or are likely to encounter later. Otherwise, separately meeting such people is a big task. Here, let me share another incident from my business journey. When I was manufacturing Sears TV and electronic components for televisions, the sales tax department did my assessment after 6-7 years. This late assessment made me anxious as the previous few year's reviews were in the red. And the enormous amount of sales tax refund was pending.

During that course, I attended a meeting with the Commissioner of Industries, who knew me and I had met at several other conferences. In that meeting, I mentioned this problem, and he immediately suggested that I could go and meet the Sales Tax Commissioner, his friend. So, with all the preparations and details, I met the Tax Commissioner. With this reference, it was easy to reach the Commissioner of Sales Tax . After listening to my points, he called the Assistant Sales Tax Officer handling my particular ward and requested to take my case. He also asked the officer to inform him of the progress. The Assistant Commissioner and his junior officer went through the issues and said that in 8 to 10 days, they would sort out these 7-8 cases, and if any refunds were accruing, it would be credited.

To my great relief, the task was completed within ten days. Of course, though, I was following it up every second day. I provided whatever details they required. Sales tax forms and C-forms are an essential part of your business. If you cannot collect forms, you must deposit an equal amount in the Government's treasury. Your sales profits will decrease by 10 to 12 percent, so why take an unnecessary hit?

A similar incident happened during my transactions with the two companies, Escorts and Eicher Good Earth, as they had not given the C-forms for 2-3 years. It amounted to Rs 7-8 lakh. I had a friend; we used to meet every week for a social get-together. Her husband was working as CEO of Eicher Good Earth. On one of such get-togethers, I mentioned the issue to her husband, and he immediately agreed to help. He asked if I could send somebody to collect C-forms and contact the Sales Department. I took immediate action, and my executive went to collect the forms and received them without delay.

An operational network is an internal network to manage and orient to your current demands and requirements. It is mainly based on your work to be efficiently managed and functions required for your organization., primarily internal and per your task requirements. The key contacts are entitled and non-discretionary requirements. Therefore, it becomes evident to you who is fit for the job. Hiring a chartered accountant or CPA who can take care of your finance, taxation, and excise statutory requirements to the Government as per the nature of your companies. It is easy to handle statutory requirements if you have a proprietorship or partnership company. A company secretary is required if you have a private limited or a minor concern.

For a distribution network, I required a distributor who could take up the sales of the TV and promotion of the company. In addition to a distributor, consider appointing a Sales Director or Vice President to oversee these efforts. This individual should ideally have a deeper understanding and expertise in sales and marketing than you do.

Marketing television sets directly was a challenging endeavor, despite the evident demand for televisions. While I could identify the substantial market requirements, I lacked the expertise and confidence to manage the marketing system effectively. To address this gap, I made the strategic decision to bring on board a Marketing Director, Mr. Khare (name changed for privacy). With 35 years of experience as an electronics consultant, he was the perfect fit for the role.

Recognizing that it might not always be feasible to offer high salaries for full-time positions, Mr. Khare and I came to an agreement for him to work four hours a day. Through his extensive industry connections and deep understanding, he played a key role in recruiting additional sales staff. His experience made it relatively easy for him to identify and onboard individuals with relevant industry backgrounds. He took charge of training the marketing team and implementing a comprehensive marketing system.

Together, we developed tools and charts to monitor the flow of demand and coordinate production to meet the increasing demand for TV sets. Mr. Khare also instituted a system that provided daily sales figures, along with weekly planning and growth analysis, to ensure that our marketing efforts remained on track.

As mentioned earlier, the production of a single complete TV set required almost 350 components. Given the complexity and scale of operations, it was imperative to hire a Senior Manager responsible for coordinating both inbound and outbound components, in addition to a Production Manager. The reason I am sharing this with you is to emphasize that certain expenses are necessary and should not be overlooked, as they play a crucial role in streamlining your business and enhancing your knowledge base.

I recognized that I could not manage the business single-handedly, especially if I wanted to scale it substantially. Furthermore, the presence of Mr. Khare, with his extensive network of contacts, proved to be beneficial for sourcing components and ensuring timely payment realization, which largely contributed to the company's success. These strategic hires and necessary expenses were vital in sustaining and expanding the business.

I also hired a financial expert on a part-time basis who could plan the cash flow and credit facility for the business. In addition, I received the payments in such a way that delayed payments were easily adjusted and did not hinder the business implementation and growth. The internal players have the power to grow or block. Therefore, ensure coordination and cooperation among these people to accomplish their tasks. However, the electronic industry is very tricky. I also realized that for the growth of the business, one should not buy cheap components to save money. Always put money into products that are quality tested. Secondly, a team of diligent and efficient people with proven backgrounds is essential. Employees are the business' foremost source. Therefore, you must ensure they are happy and engaged and help them harness their full potential.

Strategic Networking or Intentional Networking: Networking should always be adequately planned. This **Strategic networking is one that** can spark your development and financial freedom at a sooner or later stage. A strategic or intentional approach to networking empowers you to establish more diversified and premium relationships. It can further magnify your career, business, and client experience.

We decided to separate the Federation of Indian Women Entrepreneurs (FIWE) from the leading Federation of Small and Medium Enterprises (FISME). Initially, FIWE operated as the women's wing of FISME, but we recognized the need to establish it as a distinct entity. To do this, we had to complete the registration process separately from its parent organization, FISME.

Leveraging my networking skills, we arranged a meeting with the Lieutenant Governor and expressed our concerns about the registration delay we were facing. The Lieutenant Governor promptly intervened and contacted the relevant authorities on our behalf. Thanks to his intervention, our registration file was expedited and received VIP status within the Society Registration office. What would have normally taken several months was completed within a day or so, and we obtained our registration certificate in a day or so.

Join Your Club

We started the *Federation of Indian Women Entrepreneurs* in Delhi, with about 200 women members in the initial stage. Gradually, we decided to branch out from the Federation to different states. The local associations were affiliated with it, and nine more associations came forward from other states and became members.

The next target was to span across international territories, and the *International Federation of Women Entrepreneurs* was born, which converted into 11 associations from 11 countries. This Networking helped us grow. When I opened my office in the US in St. Louis, I was already connected to a group of women entrepreneurs. This Federation is Not Just a Meet and Greet but a Hope to Re-Meet.

With the help and activities of such associations, your networking can snowball. However, you ought to strategize every step, which means it has to be intentionally planned. I started getting invites from the embassy to celebrate their important days. Therefore, you should check, Plan, or analyze in what way strategy networking can help you. It would help if you associated with people who can be helpful to you in the future growth and development of your business.

There was a time when I wanted to take my business to the next level, from manufacturing TV components to starting my TV Manufacturing company. While discussing my objective with a family friend, a prominent industrialist, and a close friend of my husband, we learned that I needed some financial support from the bank for additional funds to increase my operations. That family friend came forward with extended help to schedule my meeting with the General Manager of the Oriental Bank of Commerce, with whom he had an excellent relationship. That offer was very crucial for my desire to start manufacturing immediately. Otherwise, my project would have been delayed. The process began after completing all the paperwork, worksheets, plans, and prospects. After a few visits, meetings, and presentations, it took 45 days; I was exhausted, but finally, my project was approved, and I immediately initiated my production plans.

The Importance of Planning and Scheduling

It is difficult, but Learn to Say No
and be relaxed with your time

Attending conferences, meeting people, and being continually visible establishes your credibility. In addition, the most prominent thought you must remember is "how can I help people," not the "me first" attitude.

This "me first" attitude can barricade you from building a relationship. A cup of coffee with a stranger helps to create value in life. As mentioned by Rick Turoczy, a TED Talk speaker, these cards, which we collect in different ways from strangers, are like connecting dots with dots. We should step back, reflect on these dots, and realize that our dots can see other connections, and by combining these dots, only you can see those dots. Sometimes building connectivity is artificial, but not everything unnatural is wrong. If this strikes a chord, have coffee and say yes to the next coffee. You connect the dots. Every person knows someone else, and that someone knows someone else. You are the only person who can see that.

Once, I was attending a meeting organized by RBI, Bombay. A person sitting next to me asked about my profession, and then he went on conversing for 10 minutes. After I told him about myself, he murmured, "Oh, she is not connected with my business. We can have dinner together to explain further how I can sell my services to you." He was hellbent on clinching the deal despite my repeated knockbacks. Finally, I had to voice a blunt no. The two takeaways from this example are, do not be a 'that' person and learn to say no.

I knew buying his services would have prevented me from accomplishing my goal and driven me off the mark.

Goal completion is the source of energy, inspiration, and motivation. However, you often bump into several hurdles en route to your goal.

When I started Sears International, my life was hectic. We collected cards from every conference, seminar, meeting, lunch, and dinner. It took a lot of work to handle that card folder, and most importantly, keeping track of all this was impossible. I had thousands of them but did not know how to arrange them. I also used the country-wise system and made different groups conference/event-wise. I tried many ways and used some apps like Snap biz cards. Gradually, after several tries and tests, things started to smoothen.

For time tracking, you can use calendars. Google Calendar is one tool that can help you be on time and track. However, if you are the one who schedules everything from dinner to daydreaming, opting for the Google calendar feature can interfere with your busy schedule.

Google Calendar can help you reclaim your time, mitigate mindless meetings, and keep everyone updated without a constant barrage of text and emails. Who knows: after learning the ins and outs of Google Calendar, you might find the time to make it to that open-mic improvement night after all?

We often waste time or use it ineffectively, but it is one essential resource we cannot buy. For accomplishing your goals and keeping yourself on track, scheduling is one way that helps you work out what you want to achieve in a day, week, or month.

How to Schedule Your Time

Remember the 80/20 Rule, also known as the Pareto Principle, which says that 80% of your results will come from 20% of your efforts. Therefore, prioritizing the tasks that contribute most of your gains is the key to maximizing efficiency.

Scheduling can be done at the start of every week or month. There are different tools to choose from. But I prefer a simple and easy way to accomplish the task of scheduling, i.e., by writing on paper or organizing time using a weekly or monthly planner.

You can choose scheduling tools, such as apps and software like Google Calendar, Todoist, or Microsoft Outlook. It depends on what suits your situation, budget, the current structure of your business, and your taste. When choosing your Plan, you must consider the most important things; for example, it has an easy data entry system that allows you to view the details you need, like the appropriate period, day/week/month, in a straightforward way.

Identify Available Time

Most CEOs of growing companies are busy planning and developing new products. So, if you are a business owner or planning to be one, you must plan and review if the marketing strategies are in place. Hire more people, meet new business connections, and work on finance. Attend meetings as they allow you to build a robust framework. We need subordinates to handle all the appointments and meetings, so you must hire an administrator. Otherwise, you will become an administrator yourself. Delegating administrative tasks is as pivotal as attending a conference. However, taking time for meeting schedules, sending emails, exchanging Scheduling, and rescheduling is a time-consuming and sometimes maddening exercise. Therefore, hiring an administrator to handle your hectic schedule is imperative. The time saved from this can be used towards more effective and fruitful outcomes like fundraising, networking, and doing things you like to do but cannot do due to lack of time.

Follow the principle of reciprocity. The instrumental mantra for successful networking gives, gives, and gives. Be aware of when you need to ask for a favor from a network member. Take advantage of every opportunity to give -and receive- regardless of whether you need help or not.

Networking is very critical for business growth and personal development. Small businesses must be mindful of addressing this issue. Networking amongst your friends, family, and business circle will support your work directly or indirectly. Attending conferences and seminars is one way to bolster your visibility. It empowers you to develop confidence in people that you are knowledgeable, experienced, and well-versed and that somebody can consult you for business or other issues. You can haul up your profile. You sometimes get a solution to your problem as the other person might have already gone through a similar situation, and you find a way to solve it. This way, you can avoid common pitfalls.

Connections multiply in the group, and these connections are handy when you are seeking some knowledge. It can work out as a referral if you have made an impression. So, it always works two ways: if someone in your network matches another person's business, you can share the details with them, and it will only strengthen your relationship.

Organizing visiting cards you exchanged during the conference with strangers will refine your Networking and confidence. Consorting with others also leads to opportunities. You can get a partnership request for your service or product. So, one should be ready to seize such opportunities.

Most importantly, it would help to surround yourself with people with the same motivation and drive as yours. With identical drive and motivation, you can move forward as a group. You have a group where you can draw energy and keep moving forward.

Networking must be strategic and planned. Attending seminars, meetings, and conferences is the best place to start networking.

Help people and help yourself to see that winning is possible. Leverage LinkedIn and different platforms to create a win-win situation.

Keep your communication short and precise. When asking for a favor, I always prefer to send a draft through my executive; it becomes easy for the other person to prepare a letter for me and send it.

Effective Scheduling

Be generous and selfish with your time, as we get 24 hours a day, but how we use/misuse every single moment decides the course of our business and life. I know many people who arrive at the office on time and work till late, but still feel they have yet to accomplish something significant at the end of the day. That is what we call mismanaging time.

History has shown that the most productive people use widely different scheduling techniques depending on their circumstances, personalities, and energy levels. Winston Churchill, for example, worked late into the night and broke his day with whiskey and naps. Toni Morrison began writing before dawn. So, there is no "one size fits all" to drive out maximum productivity regarding time management.

As the company's CEO, I must make many choices and master networking skills to sustain a vast circle network. I must choose what is essential for my business and what can be circumvented. Before going to an event, I analyze whether I am just going to a party or I have an agenda to meet some specific people who are likely to come to this function.

Stephen Covey's Management Gurus Time Management Grid effectively organizes your priorities. It differentiates between important activities and those that are urgent. You can prioritize the Most Important activities that have an outcome and lead to achieving your professional or personal goals. It will help you prioritize your time.

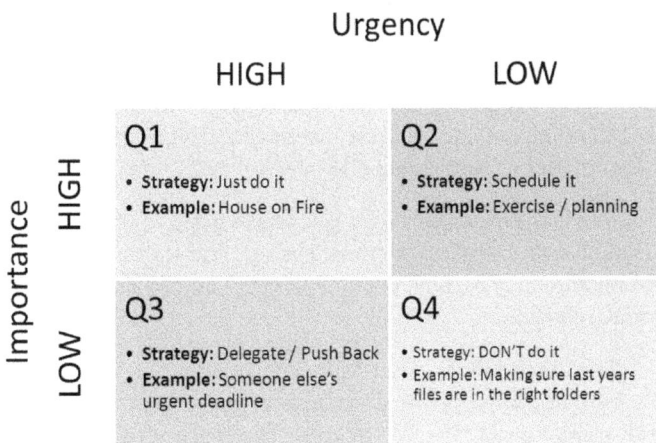

Urgency

	HIGH	LOW
Importance HIGH	**Q1** • **Strategy:** Just do it • **Example:** House on Fire	**Q2** • **Strategy:** Schedule it • **Example:** Exercise / planning
Importance LOW	**Q3** • **Strategy:** Delegate / Push Back • **Example:** Someone else's urgent deadline	**Q4** • Strategy: DON'T do it • Example: Making sure last years files are in the right folders

	URGENT	NOT URGENT
IMPORTANT	**I** • Crises • Pressing problems • Deadline-driven projects, meetings, preparations • Immediately productive activities	**II** • Preparation • Prevention • Developing Mission • Planning • Relationship building • True re-creation • Empowerment
NOT IMPORTANT	**III** • Interruptions, some phone calls • Some mail, some reports • Some meetings • Many proximate, pressing matters • Many popular activities	**IV** • Trivia, busywork • Junk mail • Some phone calls • Time wasters • "Escape" activities

Quadrant 1: Important and Urgent

To avoid serious consequences, you must deal with them immediately. Let's say you have a meeting with a fundraiser (important). It is crucial. You have to hire a Finance Director (urgent).

Quadrant 2: Important but Not Urgent

These are the events that are important but can be done later. These tasks require research and long-term strategy planning, like attending industry-specific meetings and a trade show which is Important but Not Urgent (Do later).

That is the quadrant where you should position your personal goals and spend most of your time. The goal is to work on important tasks before they become urgent and cause an imbalance in your overall schedule.

This quadrant is what will change your life over time. You will also have personal and family goals and business and professional goals. The key to **time management** is knowing your goals, prioritizing them, and focusing on tasks and activities that help you reach them.

If you are a busy entrepreneur, all your tasks should accomplish more than one thing.

Quadrant 3: Urgent but Not Important

These activities require our attention now (urgent) but do not help us achieve our goals or fulfill our mission (not important). Most Q3 tasks are interruptions from other people and often involve helping them meet their own goals and fulfill their priorities.

Quadrant 4: Neither Urgent nor Important

You know what to do with these tasks; steer clear of these activities, as these will leak out your time with no harvests.

Reasonably, quadrants 3 and 4 should be mainly eliminated.

> *"OmniFocus is a stellar tool for keeping track of outcomes and actions."*
>
> **– David Allen**

Alignment With Your Staff

There is a big misconception that doing more work makes you productive. As the CEO, you have multiple tasks to look into, and for developing your business, product for innovation, and marketing, you spend time even networking. To effectively manage your time, it is crucial to hire a personal secretary cum manager of the administration who can make calls and send emails on your behalf. All large companies follow this practice. They have a very effective coordination point, which leverages them with more free time and is effective in all areas of concern.

Very successful people allow their secretaries to email and fix appointments. I have appointed one for myself. It gives me enough time to examine the Federation of Indian Women entrepreneurs' meetings and agenda. Secondly, I can connect with people without engaging in the inescapable back and forth of scheduling. Thirdly, it also conveys to other companies that my time is important. Fourthly, having someone else fix appointments for me gives me intrinsic satisfaction. In addition, that person helps me coordinate the required changes as per the task's urgency and importance.

You can also choose software for scheduling your appointments if you do not want to spend money hiring a person. However, in India, hiring is relatively easy.

Networking for Win-Win: *Meeting People and Networking is just half way through, you have to have a long term perspective.*

I believe networking can be rewarding if you keep in mind these three aspects:

    a.   It should be an authentic connection
    b.   Timely follow-up is crucial
    c.   Keep your associates engaged

Being curious and informative helps establish your authenticity. It can convert into a meaningful connection. You will understand what people are passionate about and what part of your business will capture their interest. You can pitch in accordingly.

Networking can happen anywhere; on a train, or a plane, there is no fixed venue to network. Instead, it is most authentic in such places when you are not planning intentional networking.

Yes, social media can be a powerful tool for networking. In fact, it has revolutionized the way people connect and build relationships, both personally and professionally.

Social media platforms allow you to connect with people from all around the world. This makes it easier to network with individuals, businesses, and organizations in different countries and establish national and international connections.

Consistent and strategic use of social media can help you build a strong global brand presence, attracting customers from different parts of the world.

Dr. Shobha Dhawan, Entrepreneur, Deusch Kyosei Engineering Private Limited and Gynae Doctor

Dr. Shobha is an MBBS, DGO, and FRSH. Being an exceptional student throughout her academics, she topped her college and was accoladed with several gold medals. She began her career journey in 1978 as a Gynecologist. Shobha cherishes a rich experience of 35 years as a medical professional, also appointed as the Director at Metro Hospital. However, after practicing as a doctor for 20 years, she took on another task most professionals averted. She decided to fulfill her husband's dream and embarked on her journey as an entrepreneur. Today, she is one of the most eminent woman entrepreneurs, who has also been featured in several magazines and TV shows.

How did you start your business, and what motivated you?

My husband had plans to open a factory. We had purchased the land and made the initial 2-3 installments. The construction of the factory's basement was still underway, and operations had not yet begun. Unfortunately, during that time, I lost my husband.

In light of the circumstances, my father suggested that I continue my practice as a doctor. At that time, my son was in the 12th grade, and my father did not want him to suffer due to the loss of his father during such a crucial period. He recommended sending my son abroad for further studies. However, my son was hesitant about this idea.

Meanwhile, I started receiving offers to sell the land intended for the factory. Although I had already made all the necessary payments and extension charges, I was reluctant to part with the land. It was my husband's dream, but he was no longer with us. Making a decision became critical as time was running out.

Ultimately, I gathered all the money I received from the insurance agency, and my father also contributed some funds. With these resources, the building for the factory was constructed by my husband's company.

Once the building was ready, the next challenge was to decide what to manufacture. Initially, I considered medical products, but I did not find much market potential for them. So I abandoned that idea. Then, by chance, I came across an advertisement in The Economic Times newspaper. LML Vespa was seeking vendors for rubber and plastic parts, among other components. Considering my late husband's background in the tire industry and his connection to JK Tyre, which housed the largest rubber R&D lab in Asia, I decided to focus on manufacturing rubber parts.

Through perseverance and determination, I established the necessary infrastructure and assembled a skilled team. The process involved relentless dedication, numerous negotiations, and meticulous planning. However, each passing day fueled my determination, driven by my desire to honor my husband's dream and create a thriving business.

As I navigated the complexities of production, quality control, and vendor management, I fully immersed myself in understanding the intricacies of rubber parts manufacturing. Seeking guidance from industry experts, attending workshops, and building a network of mentors became instrumental in overcoming the challenges I faced.

Over time, my factory flourished. I witnessed the growth of our customer base and the increasing demand for our products. The satisfaction of seeing my husband's dream come to life and experiencing the rewards of my resilience was immeasurable. But beyond the financial success, what truly warmed my heart was the impact my efforts had on my son.

Initially hesitant about studying abroad, my son witnessed firsthand the dedication and determination that I poured into the factory. He observed the fruits of my labor and grasped the importance of pursuing dreams, even in the face of adversity. Inspired by my resilience, he embraced the opportunity and embarked on his own educational journey abroad, fueled by the belief that hard work and perseverance could lead to anything.

Reflecting on my life, I realize that my path as an entrepreneur extends far beyond merely running a factory. It serves as a testament to the strength of the human spirit, the power of resilience, and the bonds that unite us as a family.

In conclusion, my life's journey has been a transformation from a grieving widow to a determined entrepreneur. It showcases the unwavering spirit within each of us, urging us to embrace life's challenges and transform them into opportunities. By sharing my experiences, I hope to inspire and empower others, particularly women who have faced adversity, to step into their power and fearlessly pursue their dreams.

I hope my journey serves as a reminder that we have the ability to achieve greatness, even in the face of loss and uncertainty.

But it must have been tough, as you were a doctor and had zero experience in manufacturing. How did you manage?

Indeed, turning my determination into a tangible reality was far from easy. It was the year 1997-98, a period when women entrepreneurs faced limited endorsement. My first step was to acquire the necessary knowledge and expertise. I reached out to Mr. Singhania, the owner of JK Tyre, and humbly requested his assistance with the technological aspects. To my surprise, he generously agreed to help me. When I called him, he happened to be having lunch and must have wondered who this lady doctor was. After explaining the connection between my late husband and him, he assured me that he would recommend my name to the Vice President of vendor development.

Traveling to Kanpur, I had the opportunity to meet the Vice President, who graciously shared some drawings of the parts that needed to be manufactured. However, lacking the machinery at that time, I decided to make use of the compounding residues from JK Tyre. Outsourcing the mixing process, I diligently prepared some samples. This meticulous process took several months to complete. When I contacted the Vice President again, I was informed that he had been transferred, and Mr. Laxmi Narayan had taken over his position. Undeterred, I arranged a meeting with Mr. Laxmi, accompanied by my son. I shared the background of my situation and presented the samples I had prepared. To my surprise and delight, by 4 PM that day, I received Vendor Registration and an order worth Rs. 10 lakhs per month. Mr. Laxmi revealed that he would not have typically granted Vendor Registration to just any established company unless they were ISO-certified and a 2-wheeler supplier. However, he made an exception in my case. I expressed my heartfelt gratitude and returned home. The following day, I visited the bank.

During that time, the evaluated value of my building's property stood at Rs. 82 lakhs. With determination, I approached the bank to request a loan, but initially faced resistance due to being a woman and a doctor. However, I persisted and ultimately convinced them to grant me a loan of Rs. 6 lakhs. Though it was a relatively small amount, it allowed me to fulfill the requirements of the first order.

Meanwhile, Mr. Laxmi Narayan visited the site. Unfortunately, at that point, I had not yet procured any machinery; only the building stood. However, with steady progress, the construction of the building was completed, obtaining all the necessary certifications. I then began the process of setting up my plant.

How did you acquire the necessary business knowledge?

I gained business knowledge through the support and guidance provided by JK Tyre. They assisted me with project reports and advised me on which machines to purchase.

How important was networking in your business growth and life?

Networking has played a crucial role in my life and has been instrumental in helping me reach new heights. It is essential for business success. Networking is incredibly important for business growth, and it plays a vital role in an individual's professional life.

Networking holds great significance. In fact, our lives are interconnected through networking. We currently have 32 international partners. For many years, I hosted parties where members of Parliament and even Cabinet Ministers would attend. We also organized corporate dinners where senior individuals from various industries, including the tyre and automobile sectors, would participate.

At what point did you realize that your company needed to grow and required additional capital?

I felt the need for growth and additional capital throughout the journey. In the initial stages of my first company, I relied solely on a hydraulic press and gathered knowledge about rubber technology through various books. Friends of my late husband also visited my factory and offered assistance with the technology. It was during this time that I discovered the potential of rubber injection molding. However, the cost of injection molding was quite high, around Rs. 80 lakhs, while the hydraulic press cost around Rs. 10 lakhs. Despite the challenges, I decided to invest in injection molding technology as I believed in its viability and potential. To finance this expansion, I sought capital from SIDBI (Small Industries Development Bank of India).

What was the turnover of your company, and how much funding did you request from SIDBI and in which year?

The turnover of my company was approximately Rs. 50 lakhs. We applied for a loan from SIDBI sometime after the year 2000. Initially, I used the loan to purchase a needle and a mixer. Subsequently, I sought further funding for acquiring injection molding machines, and currently, we have four of them. I aimed to adopt advanced technologies and attain relevant accreditations. For the SIDBI loan, I submitted documents requesting a loan amount ranging from Rs. 50 lakhs to 1 crore.

As your business has now expanded significantly, did you approach any Angel Investor or Venture Capitalist?

No, I did have discussions with people regarding potential investments, but I decided against involving Angel Investors or Venture Capitalists. I felt that such arrangements would result in them having control over my company. Therefore, apart from the bank, I do not have any other investors.

Key Takeaways

- ♗ Join alumni groups, professional associations, and interest communities.
- ♗ Identify individuals who can efficiently support your routine task.
- ♗ Question your three networking plans and work on it.
- ♗ Plan and identify people who can contribute to your long-term goals.
- ♗ Utilize associations to connect with professionals such as bankers, lawyers, and government officials.
- ♗ Learn to say 'no' and prioritize tasks based on the 80/20 Rule.
- ♗ Be generous and selfish with your time; manage it effectively.
- ♗ Networking should be based on authentic connections rather than transactional relationships.
- ♗ Social media platforms facilitate connections with individuals, businesses, and organizations worldwide.

CHAPTER 7

Being Yourself – 'Not a Quitter'

"There are two ways to live: you can live as if nothing is a miracle; you can live as if everything is a miracle."

– Albert Einstein

Strike for the Perfect Balance Between Your Personal and Professional Life

When multiple things are happening on the personal and professional front, you may feel uneasy and perturbed by the issues. There could be scenarios where you may feel guilty. Specifically for women, motherhood is the sacrifice equation, and it is so deeply ingrained in our minds that even highly professionally centered women get affected by it when 100% of their time is not given to the family. Though she may be outwardly defying to be family-oriented and be a solid professional, deep inside her heart, it may not be the same. She keeps trying her best to balance the two. She is a hard-working, jostling mother, thriving on the hugs and kisses of her children, and works as a boss in the office.

"The Associated Chambers of Commerce and Industry (ASSOCHAM) conducted a survey in 2015 and found that a large number of professional women are abandoning becoming full-time mothers. They found it challenging to raise children and pursue a career, which is a complex and challenging task; Assocham interacted with over 400 mothers in 10 cities aged 25 to 30 to find out about their employment situation after Motherhood. The survey, conducted from March to April, highlighted that the majority of these women intend to re-enter the workforce once their children begin attending school. However, a significant number expressed concerns about returning to their previous jobs due to fears of facing discrimination.

Most of the respondents held master's degrees in various fields, indicating their high level of education. Nonetheless, conflicting priorities emerged as the primary reason for their decision to quit their jobs.

This survey sheds light on the choices made by first-time mothers in India and the challenges they face in juggling their professional and personal lives. It simply highlights the need for supportive policies and inclusive work environments that enable women to pursue their careers while fulfilling their responsibilities as mothers.

According to a 2013 World Bank study, only 27% of women aged over 15 were found to be working in India. This percentage is the lowest rate of women's participation in any workforce among the BRICS (Brazil, Russia, India, China, and South Africa) countries. The figure is the highest in China, at 64%."

2024- 14th Global Economic Summit,
South African Ambassador & Delegate

I would like to share my dilemma. One day, while I was in my factory, it was 5 PM, which was my usual time to leave the office. At 4 PM, I received a call from home. My mother-in-law informed me that my son was running high fever and desperately wanted to see me. This is when a child craves the magical touch of their mother. I was about to leave when a sales tax inspector arrived unexpectedly for an inspection. I was mentally unprepared for this surprise visit, but I had no choice but to provide him with the documents he requested.

Time seemed to be rapidly ticking away as he went through the papers, and every passing minute felt like a ticking time bomb.. The drive home would also take 45 minutes, so I decided to answer the call. I pleaded with the inspector, explaining that my son was unwell, and I had to leave. He appeared visibly frustrated and clearly displeased with my prioritizing my personal situation over his work. However, in my desperation, I locked my cabin, handed the books to my accountant, and asked him to assist the inspector and answer his questions. I found myself torn between two urgent matters – an irritated inspector on one side and my son's health on the other.

In the end, I chose the most critical matter, driven by my maternal instinct to tend to my son's well-being. It was a challenging situation, and I had to manage my emotions, including feelings of anger, frustration, and helplessness. Balancing the roles of being a good boss and an efficient mother can be chaotic at times.

Question Yourself About Your Emotional and Mental Wellness

But soon, I realized that such situations would recur, so instead of becoming emotional and uneasy, I should be able to handle them smartly and in a relaxed way. This is called **personal ecology**. It means maintaining balance, pacing, and efficiency to sustain our energy over a lifetime.

I was not as perfect as my husband is in managing time. Maintaining balance, pacing, and efficiency are key factors for sustaining energy throughout one's lifetime. These aspects play a crucial role in managing various responsibilities and commitments while avoiding burnout and exhaustion. Let me further explain.

By achieving a sense of balance, individuals can allocate time and energy to different areas of their lives, such as work, family, personal well-being, and hobbies. This involves setting priorities, establishing boundaries, and recognizing the importance of self-care. Striking a healthy balance allows individuals to dedicate sufficient time and attention to each aspect without neglecting their own needs.

Pacing is another essential aspect of energy sustainability. It involves understanding personal limits, managing workload, and avoiding excessive stress or overexertion.

Successful pacing will create a balance between your energy and activity levels, increase your confidence with exercise, maintain your motivation with activity, reduce fatigue and improve performance.

Efficiency is epoch-making for optimizing productivity and conserving energy. It involves adopting effective strategies and techniques to accomplish tasks in a streamlined and organized manner. We have already discussed this in Chapter 6: Networking. This may include prioritizing tasks, delegating responsibilities when possible, at the same time, leveraging technology and tools. This helps in continuous improvement of work processes. By working efficiently, individuals can maximize output while minimizing wasted time and energy.

Incorporating balance, pacing, and efficiency into daily routines and long-term planning can contribute to sustained energy levels over a lifetime. It enables individuals to lead fulfilling lives, pursue their goals, and maintain overall well-being while effectively managing their energy resources.

Let me share some examples of how the critical components of personal ecology can be practiced:

1. Physical well-being:

   - Engaging in regular exercise, such as walking, jogging, or yoga.
   - Maintaining a balanced and nutritious diet, incorporating fruits, vegetables, and whole grains.
   - Prioritizing sufficient sleep and rest to rejuvenate the body.
   - Practicing stress management techniques, such as deep breathing or meditation.

2. Mental and emotional well-being:

   - Practicing mindfulness or meditation to cultivate present-moment awareness.
   - Seeking therapy or counseling when needed to address emotional challenges.
   - Participating in social or community groups to expand social connections.
   - Engaging in active listening and effective communication with loved ones.
   - Supporting and helping others, fostering a sense of belonging and community.
   - Surrounding oneself with positive and supportive relationships.

3. Purpose and fulfillment:

   - Reflecting on personal values and aligning daily actions with them.
   - Setting meaningful goals that provide a sense of purpose and working towards achieving them.
   - Engaging in volunteer work or community service to contribute to causes that matter. This helps in channeling your energies in a positive direction.
   - Exploring personal interests and passions to cultivate a sense of fulfillment.

4. Relationships and social connections:

   - Nurturing relationships with family and friends through regular communication and quality time together.

- Participating in social or community groups to expand social connections.
- Engaging in active listening and effective communication with loved ones.
- Supporting and helping others, fostering a sense of belonging and community.

5. Environmental consciousness:

- Practicing sustainable habits, such as recycling, reducing waste, and conserving energy and teaching the same to your children.
- Connecting with nature through activities like hiking, gardening, or nature walks.
- Educating oneself about environmental issues and supporting environmentally friendly initiatives.
- Promoting sustainability within the workplace or community.

6. Self-reflection and self-awareness:

- Journaling or keeping a personal diary to reflect on thoughts, emotions, and experiences.
- Engaging in regular self-assessment to identify strengths, weaknesses, and areas for personal growth.
- Seeking feedback from trusted individuals to gain insights into personal development areas.
- Engaging in personal development activities, such as reading self-help books or attending workshops.

Surround yourself with the people who support you and see the potential in your project instead of seeing all the obstacles it will face. But luckily, I had my mother-in-law to support me at home and a very understanding husband to take care of matters when he was at home in my absence. Nurturing relationships with family and friends through regular communication and quality time together matters a lot.

Running a business is quite stressful; it is a full-time sport with a few free hours, despite you being so efficient. In the first year of business, you are passionate and work nonstop. When I used to go to social gatherings, I would look for somebody with whom I could discuss some issue or something related to business. I was least interested in talking to women with nothing else to chat about besides their families, clothes, and jewelry. The priorities of business were so overpowered in mind that 24 hours your focus is only on how and what to do to increase your business.

After a few years, I realized the importance of reconnecting with the person inside me. It became clear that I must spend time with friends, share laughter, and attend lunches and parties. So, I started making an effort to join association meetings and luncheons with friends. While there were times when I could not make it, I tried my best to show up for these gatherings.

These experiences helped rejuvenate not just my body but also my mind and soul. It reminded me that life beyond work deserves as much attention as product development in the pipeline. Being part of social or community groups allowed me to expand my social connections and ensured that I stayed engaged and connected. Active listening and effective communication with loved ones played a major role, as did supporting and helping others, nestling a sense of belonging and community.

I joined a singing group with some friends, and we made it a monthly tradition to get together for singing sessions and enjoy a meal together. We must constantly remind ourselves that we work to live and not live to work. I realized that however efficient and effective moms we are, we must work to feel good with the family. Carving out a non-working time from your jam-packed calendar is a blessing in disguise.

When we, the businesswomen at the Federation of Indian Women Entrepreneurs (FIWE), discussed it, we realized that having social and physical activity along with our business requirements is indispensable.

I met Sulekha in the FIWE group. She is a fashion designer and a big supplier of garments to the Johnsons. She has been running a successful business despite being a mother of two daughters. Out of her busy schedule, she does yoga every morning and spends fixed hours of her morning time with her husband. If her team tries to call her and her phone is switched off, they know very well that Surekha is with her family, and she should not be bothered. She has made it a practice to balance her personal and professional life. This involves setting priorities, establishing boundaries, and recognizing the importance of self-care.

Delegating work is one such way to find time for your critical thinking and planning. I started sending my salespersons to exhibitions and other places to check the launch of new products and ultimately work on their details. Delegating home chores to our home staff is essential. India is one such country, where the facilities to keep an affordable staff at home are possible. This way, I could get some free time to pick up my daughter from school and treat her to ice cream, and go with her to a birthday party of her schoolmate once in a while. Hence, apart from my professional life, there is a boatload of cherishing moments in my memory folder.

Practice Improving Your Game

I made it a point to practice yoga every morning once the kids left for school. I also do pranayama for 20 minutes, which **relieves** my stress. These activities are a part of my routine, so I make time for them and focus on my business and family efficiently. So much so that when I went on frequent trips abroad", I used to do my yoga and pranayama before going for breakfast and meetings. It became a perpetual requirement for physical and mental fitness. I used to do it for ten minutes if time did not permit me. Further, I have always been a family-oriented person.

Men attribute their success to themselves; women attribute their success to other factors. That is probably why a lack of self-esteem gets ingrained in women.

Being active in the Association and also being a President of it, speaking at gatherings of conferences, meetings, colleges, and government meetings, had a perfectly profound effect on me. Earlier, I used to stutter, feel hesitant, and always feel doubtful about my capabilities. But after the continuous practice of public speaking, I gained confidence and courage. I wish we had coaches then who could teach us how to deliver speeches and feel motivated. Now women have a lot of such opportunities to express themselves through social media, be it through Facebook, LinkedIn, Instagram, or YouTube. Also, coaches are available for public speaking and blog writing.

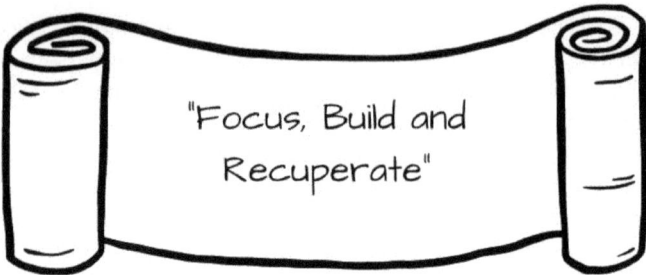

> "Focus, Build and Recuperate"

I have realized that most women CEOs I have talked to are grounded. Our power comes from within. Our yoga classes help charge through us, not for being strident.

Practicing yoga for the past 30 years has taught me valuable life lessons. In yoga, mastering challenging poses like the headstand (ShirshAsana) or Tripod Pose Crow (Kak Asana) requires working on various sub-asanas and gradually progressing towards the final pose. Through consistent practice, you can achieve these advanced poses and even perform a headstand without any support, which is a phenomenal accomplishment.

Yoga also imparts leadership skills. When you practice yoga, there is no comparison with others, and your guru focuses on guiding you without criticizing your failures. This approach is akin to leading a team in business. You can put yourself in the shoes of your employees, just like you did when learning yoga. It teaches us to push our limits incrementally and consistently, ultimately leading to success. Embracing the process and finding joy in both trying and succeeding are compelling.

I recall my initial attempts at the headstand, where I was afraid of falling and getting hurt. I soon realized I was overemphasizing one side, causing an imbalance. With conscious adjustments and gradual modifications, I eventually achieved a perfect headstand. This experience mirrors the approach needed in business—maintaining a healthy balance, dedicating ample time and attention to each aspect, and ensuring that personal well-being is not neglected. I recall my yoga teacher recommending a deep breathing exercise during the COVID-19 pandemic. It involved taking a deep inhale and holding the breath for as long as possible before exhaling. With daily practice, I noticed that my breath-holding capacity increased pressingly. This exercise was of great consequence during the pandemic, as it helped strengthen the lungs, making them more resilient in the face of infection.

You need not be perfect on the first stance. But it is important to try and do something, and then you can modify your business practices.

In addition to yoga, I also incorporate meditation into my daily routine. I have a deep connection with nature, so I spend a few minutes in my garden, where I admire the beauty of flowers and even engage in conversations with them. This ritual provides me with the inspiration and energy needed to kick-start my day. I find immense joy in the melodious symphony of chirping birds, the powerful calls of peacocks, and the soothing tunes of cuckoos. It is a rejuvenating experience that reconnects me with the natural world, offering solace and tranquility amidst the hustle and bustle of everyday life.

So, in a nutshell, my approach is to keep improving and refining your skills. Just as playing against stronger opponents elevates your level of competition, embracing these practices allows for continuous personal growth and development.

Understand that investors focus on two key factors: the achievements or milestones you have reached and the momentum your business is gaining. Even if you have fewer accomplishments, the speed at which you are progressing can make up for it. Just like a sports player, be prepared to actively participate and make your mark in the game of entrepreneurship.

The four components of mental wellness can be summarized as follows:

Emotional Wellness: This aspect focuses on your emotional state, including self-acceptance, self-esteem, resilience, and your ability to manage and express emotions effectively.

Social Wellness: Social wellness pertains to your interactions with others and the quality of your relationships. It involves maintaining positive and supportive connections with friends, family, and the community.

Financial Wellness: Financial wellness is related to your financial health and stability. It encompasses your ability to manage finances, budget effectively, save for the future, and reduce financial stress.

Physical Wellness: Physical wellness in the context of mental health involves taking care of your body through regular exercise, a balanced diet, and sufficient sleep. Physical well-being can have a significant impact on your mental state.

These components collectively contribute to mental wellness and overall well-being, ensuring a balanced and healthy state of mind.

> *"Being in control of your life and having realistic expectations about your day-to-day challenges are the keys to stress management, perhaps the most important ingredient to living a happy, healthy, and rewarding life."*

> **— Marilu Henner, Actress**

Not a Quitter

As parents, we strive to provide the best for our children. In our fast-paced world, fathers may sometimes believe they are exceeding their own fathers in their parental efforts. They may engage in activities like playing with their kids or enjoying a sports game together, actions they believe surpass their own upbringing. These moments lead them to assess themselves as exemplary fathers.

Conversely, modern mothers may have a different perspective. They might feel that they are not living up to the standards set by their own mothers. This sentiment can trigger self-doubt and a sense of inadequacy as mothers, leading them to question their interactions with their children and experience feelings of guilt.

Some men may boast about their professional achievements, such as reaching the position of CEO through their hard work. When I hear such boasts, I cannot help but think about switching roles. I wonder how they would handle enduring 24 hours of labor pain or going through a cesarean section. Returning from the hospital and caring for a newborn while also looking after a 3-4-year-old, all the while running a business, can be an incredibly challenging and underappreciated role. It is a multifaceted task that requires significant physical and emotional effort, and sometimes, we may stumble in the process.

Balancing the demands of a career with the responsibilities of motherhood brings unique challenges, distinct from those encountered in white or blue-collar jobs. These challenges take on a different form for women who aspire to be CEOs or already hold such positions. Their concerns extend beyond issues like pay equity and maternity leave; their primary challenge revolves around maintaining competitiveness in the workplace. What makes this particularly challenging is that the most critical phase for business growth often aligns with the time when they also want to have a baby.

Understand that the struggles faced by mothers, especially those aspiring to be CEOs, are in a category of their own. Simultaneously pursuing business growth and motherhood creates a complex and demanding situation that requires understanding and support from both family and society. It is a unique odyssey that deserves recognition and respect.

There are specific jobs that are not part-time or temporary. There are 24-hour jobs like at TV stations, hospitals, restaurants, or running a business. The woman must decide how to manage, collaborate with her partner, live in a joint family, or some other suitable alternative. One must develop specific ways to hush the negative thoughts and comparisons that play continuously throughout the day.

This tug-of-war between work and home will continue. Therefore, one must ask, "What do I want the most?" When at work, I ask myself what I enjoy the most. At home, I ask myself whether my family needs me more, and I work out accordingly. Do I need to see my daughter's play performance in school, or can I miss it for another meeting?

I could ask my mother to plan to go and watch her first dance performance. I do her craft project together with her; it is okay even if I miss it some days.

But whenever you remember all your mistakes, you feel deflated. You have to make tough choices. You must know yourself and set your rules accordingly. You should train your mind to switch from victim-type thinking to take-the-charge-type thinking and deal with it. One essential approach is to prioritize what matters the most and set personal rules accordingly. Rather than dwelling on negative thoughts and comparisons, taking 100 percent responsibility for one's actions can lead to a positive shift in mindset.

During a challenging phase in our lives, my husband and I were experiencing difficulties, and I found relief from my struggles and mental tension when I decided to take 100 percent responsibility for my actions instead of blaming my partner. There was a time when my husband's work commitments took precedence for a while, and I chose to take charge and find moments to connect with him, such as having morning tea together whenever we were in Delhi.

This revolutionary approach brought about a positive shift in my thought process. Both my husband, Praveen, and I embraced this mindset and actively worked on it. I had chosen to balance the roles of a CEO and a mother, and both were vital positions. It meant avoiding the easier route of blaming and choosing to cease self-inflicted harm by taking proactive actions to improve our situation.

As a young college girl, I was carefree, but after marriage, my feelings took a 180-degree turn. I realized that challenging stretches in life could persist, whether for a day, a week, or a few months. It was this realization that pushed me to take charge of my own happiness and strive for better days.

I was busy setting up my export business and had to visit the US at least five to six times a year. My husband was already busy with his consultancy job and had to go to the Delhi office and sometimes to Dubai to inspect the steel plant. So, there have been numerous times when we both were traveling. However, throughout my life, we savored morning tea together whenever we were in Delhi. Usually, my husband prepares the morning tea. Over tea, we discuss various issues related to our respective businesses, his assignments, children, and family matters.

There was a phase when I started missing that morning tea as my husband got busy with the new assignment. Afterward, His travel plans became quite frequent. The expansion of the factory in Sri Lanka was overly occupying him. Due to this over-occupation, there needed to be more attention to work than to me. That continued for a long time. And then there was a silence between both of us.

One morning, I found myself feeling lazy and contemplated avoiding going to the factory. So, I made a call to my office and informed them that I would arrive in the afternoon, following lunch. I thought about visiting a friend to break the routine. However, the concept of taking 100 percent responsibility came to mind, and I pondered how my actions might differ if I fully owned the responsibility. So, I decided to call my husband and inquire if he was available for lunch.

To my delight, he promptly replied with a "yes." We enjoyed lunch together, and during our meal, we reminisced about our past adventures. We talked about the places we used to visit, how we often arrived late for movies, typically just before intermission, and how we loved to take detours on our way to Shimla, like turning toward Kasauli. Despite our busy schedules and two kids, we marveled at how we now successfully manage our high-profile careers, although our trips to the hills have become less frequent. Whenever young entrepreneurs ask me for advice, I suggest they take 100 percent responsibility and reflect on what they want the most while making a crucial decision.

An entrepreneur, Ms Annu Aggarwal, had a retail store, and the lease was due, which she was looking forward to getting renewed. Every day, she used to reach home late because of work overload. Her son and daughter always complained, "Mum, you are not there when we return from school." This grievance was hitting her like a bombshell. She started feeling guilty. She deliberated over what she wanted the most. And then, she decided to take 100 percent responsibility for being there for the kids. She realized that she could revisit her business later while currently prioritizing her kids. A woman analyzed that if she takes a pause a few years, later she can either restart the business or join a corporation at the post where she would be free to work and make decisions like an entrepreneur. But currently, her kids are her number one priority. And she did not get the lease renewed.

Both my husband and I were frequently traveling for business, and it reached the point where we sometimes only managed to meet at the airport. This continued for at least 4 to 5 years until I felt the need to reevaluate our situation.

Engaging family members in the business can be a creative way to integrate work and personal life. Involving my son in inspecting leather goods and my daughter in contributing ideas created a supportive and enriching environment.

Ultimately, releasing the burden of guilt and accepting the challenges of balancing work and family can be a liberating experience for working women. Each individual must discover their unique approach to effectively manage responsibilities while pursuing their passions. Whenever I visited my parents, I realized that ***you can take out a woman from the company but cannot take out the company from a woman.***

I sincerely believe that the greatest gift we can give this generation of working women is to "get rid of guilt" and embrace those tricky things around us, allowing us to do what we love.

The key takeaway is that there is no one-size-fits-all solution to this juggling act. It requires introspection, communication with one's partner and family, and setting clear priorities to find a harmonious balance between work and home life. By taking 100 percent responsibility for decisions and focusing on what truly matters, working women can navigate their professional and personal worlds with greater fulfillment and success.

Achieving work-life balance can be challenging for any entrepreneur, including women entrepreneurs. However, some strategies can help women entrepreneurs prioritize their personal lives while managing their business responsibilities. Let me share some tips for women entrepreneurs to achieve work-life balance:

1. Set clear boundaries. Establish boundaries between work and personal life. Define specific working hours and try to stick to them. Avoid bringing work into personal time and vice versa. Never discuss business in your bedroom with your husband, limit it to the dining table only.
2. Identify tasks that can be delegated or outsourced to free up your time. Hiring competent employees or outsourcing certain functions can give you more time for personal commitments.
3. Set priorities for both work and personal life. Use time management techniques, which have been explained in Chapter 6, such as making to-do lists, setting deadlines, and breaking tasks into smaller manageable chunks. Focus on high-value tasks that align with your business goals and personal priorities.

4. Build a support network. Seek support from family, friends, and mentors who can understand and support your entrepreneurial journey. Delegate household chores and responsibilities to family members or consider hiring help to alleviate some non-work-related burdens.

5. To maintain a strong relationship with your husband, try to avoid unnecessary conflicts and arguments, as both of you may have different perspectives. Be compromise-ready and prioritize his preferences in your personal space to nurture a harmonious and happy relationship. It is a primal bond in your life that deserves understanding and patience.

6. Leverage tools that enable remote work and collaboration. Embracing flexible work arrangements can help create a better work-life balance. Allow your employees to work from home periodically. It boosts their confidence in the organization. Working from home has created flexible working hours for employees.

7. Take care of yourself. Prioritize self-care, including physical exercise, healthy eating, and sufficient rest. Personal health care is essential for maintaining productivity and overall well-being.

8. Set realistic expectations. Give yourself the necessary time to accomplish tasks within a reasonable timeframe. Refrain from taking on too many commitments, and do not hesitate to decline tasks or projects that do not align with your primary goals. Overcommitting has been a personal challenge for me, as I tend to push my limits repeatedly. Break free from such habits and recognize that they do not define your personality.

9. Schedule downtime and personal activities. This entails spending time with loved ones, pursuing hobbies, or engaging in relaxation techniques; incorporate these activities into your schedule. Block off time for activities that you enjoy and that recharge you mentally and emotionally.

Leave your mobile completely at family dinner time. Remember that achieving work-life balance is an ongoing process that may require adjustments and fine-tuning. Continually align with your personal and professional goals, reassessing your priorities and making essential conscious choices.

Exercises and Practices

Remember, finding the right balance is a personal journey, and it may require experimentation and adjustments. Choose exercises and practices that resonate with you and integrate them into your routine consistently to promote work-life balance.

Self-reflection and self-awareness: Journaling or maintaining a personal diary can be a valuable practice to contemplate your thoughts, emotions, and experiences. It allows you to evaluate what is and is not working in your life and helps you identify steps to align your actions with your desired balance. Here are some suggestions you may follow:

Mindfulness meditation and breathing exercises: Take a few minutes each day to practice mindfulness meditation. Sit in a quiet space, focus on your breath, and bring your attention to the present moment.

Physical exercise: Engage in regular physical exercise, such as jogging, yoga, or strength training.. Find activities that you enjoy and make them a consistent part of your routine.

Time-blocking: Use time-blocking techniques to allocate specific time slots for work, personal activities, and rest.

Take periodic breaks from digital devices and technology: Designate specific times or days when you disconnect from emails, social media, and other online activities. Use this time to engage in activities that promote relaxation and face-to-face interactions.

– eg. Saturday and Wednesday

Creative outlets: This could include painting, writing, playing a musical instrument, singing or dancing or any other creative hobby that brings you joy and helps you disconnect from work-related stress.

Set boundaries: between work and personal life: Communicate your availability and preferred methods of communication to colleagues and clients.

Social connections: Nurture and maintain relationships with family, friends, and colleagues.

In the quest for self-reflection and self-awareness, we find the power to transform ourselves and our lives. As we continue to explore the depths of our thoughts and emotions, we unlock the potential for growth and balance. With each step, we come closer to understanding our true selves and living a life aligned with our most profound desires and aspirations.

Dr. Uma Sharma, MBBS and DGO
from Lady Hardinge, Delhi

Dr. Uma Sharma, MBBS and DGO from Lady Hardinge, Delhi University has 35 years of rich experience in the field of OBST and Gynae. She is the chairperson of the Kailash Group of Hospitals Noida, Greater Noida, Delhi (Deepak Memorial Hospital), Naturopathy Institute and Kailash Health Village Noida and Dehradun.

She has conducted over 100 training programs and delivered numerous lectures on gynecology and obstetrics. She was recognized with the Shiromani Mahila Udyami Award by the Noida Mahila Udyam Sansthan. She is married to Dr. Mahesh Sharma, a Member of Parliament and former Minister of State for Tourism and Culture, Civil Aviation, Environment, and Forest in the Government of India.

How do you manage the demands of your medical practice while maintaining a healthy work-life balance?

Managing the demands of a medical practice while maintaining a healthy work-life balance can be challenging, but it is possible with careful planning and execution. For this, I follow a few routine practices like I set boundaries between my work life and my personal life. I try to delegate my tasks which helps to free up my time as well as give others more opportunities. One of the most important things in my field is to learn how to say NO, as all my patients are important but I have to work within my own capacity so that I can work efficiently and am not exerted too. Lastly, I take good care of myself by taking a proper diet, getting enough sleep and going for a walk every day.

What strategies or techniques do you employ to prevent work from consuming your personal life?

My work has been my profession as well as my passion. Although I love my work but still to keep my personal life different, I take breaks to go on vacations. I have a routine that I follow each day which helps me to stay on track and avoid getting overwhelmed, and I have a great support system of friends and family who helps me to stay grounded and balanced.

Do you have any specific routines or boundaries that you have set to ensure work-life balance?

Yes, I do have a very strict routine that I follow every day; I have a set working schedule from Monday to Saturday; I work from 10 AM to 2 PM, then take a break and again start working from 6 PM to 8 PM. Only in cases of emergencies do I make an exception. I take breaks whenever I feel tired and in that time, I visit my patients in recovery which motivates me and gives me a feeling of accomplishment to see them healthy.

How do you prioritize your time between your medical business and personal/family commitments?

I have a big family as well as a busy profession, it can sometimes be quite challenging to balance my work and family commitments, but on the brighter side, I have a very supportive family, who understands the needs of my work life which relieves me from a lot of pressure. But whenever my family needs me, I do not think twice about being there for them even if I have to rely on my colleagues for my work.

Have you faced any challenges in achieving work-life balance as a doctor entrepreneur, and how have you overcome them?

The medical field is very demanding. As an entrepreneur and a doctor, I have to put very long hours and immense energy into my work life. This can be quite stressful and sometimes takes a toll on my health. Therefore, I make sure that I exercise daily, take time outs whenever I am under a lot of stress and practice yoga, which helps me to have good mental health and see everything in a positive light.

Are there any specific technologies, tools, or apps that you utilize to streamline your work and create more time for personal activities?

I am not very tech-savvy; I still believe in more traditional approaches. Although the use of mails, WhatsApp, etc. has made it easier for me to converse with my patients and colleagues about any issues or queries. It has helped me to be present with my family and friends as well as be there for my patients.

Do you delegate tasks or responsibilities to others to help manage your workload and free up time for your personal life? If so, how do you decide what to delegate?

Delegating tasks does not mean running from your responsibilities but also giving opportunities to others. I understood this fact after I reached a certain position in my life where I felt if I did not delegate my work, then how would my juniors learn? It even helps me to free up some time for myself, which helps me to relax and relieves the pressure on me. To delegate the work, I tend to see the skills of the person I am giving the task and responsibility to, I mostly do the critical work on my own and give less critical tasks to others so that they learn step by step and I do make sure that the other person is also available for the work as I do not like to put them under any sort of pressure they cannot handle.

How do you handle the stress and pressures that come with being a doctor entrepreneur, and how does it impact your work-life balance?

Being a doctor entrepreneur is very stressful and demanding. There are many pressures to perform well, both in terms of patient care and business. It is very difficult and challenging to make crucial decisions when so many people are looking up to you and are dependent on your decisions. This can be very stressful and sometimes leads to anger outbursts which I try to control with my daily yoga practices. For this, I take time out, do not react instantly, and deal with the problem by myself and then talk to others about it. Doing yoga has helped me to cope with these stressful situations for the past several years and thus helps me to keep a healthy work-life balance.

Have you made any significant changes or adjustments to your career or business to improve

your work-life balance? If so, what were they and how did they impact you?

I have not made any big changes in my work life, just a few small adjustments like I have started keeping realistic goals. I am not afraid to ask for help when needed or say no to requests that will overextend me.

Can you share any personal experiences or stories where maintaining work-life balance has been particularly challenging, and how you navigated through them?

In the year 1990, it had just been two years since I had started my medical practice. It was the most crucial time of my life when I was growing professionally. However, on a vacation with my family, I met with a very bad car accident due to which I had to take a very long break from my work. I was exhausted from all the surgeries I was going through, and it had taken a bad toll on my mental health too. Getting back to my work life was challenging, but I knew that I had to do it.

I started by taking things slowly. I worked for a few hours at first, and then gradually increased my hours. I also started seeing a therapist to help me process my emotions and deal with the trauma of the accident.

It took some time, but eventually, I was able to get back to my full-time job. I was still tired, and I had to be careful not to overdo it. But I was also grateful to be back at work, and I was determined to make the most of it.

I learned a lot from my experience. I learned that it is important to take care of myself, both physically and mentally. I also learned that I ought to have a strong support system. My family and friends were there for me every step of the way, and they helped me get through the tough times.

I am glad that I could return to my work life. It holds substance for me, and it is where my strengths lie. I am also pleased that I could learn from my experience and emerge as a stronger individual.

Key Takeaways

- What are the 3 things I can do to combat my stress?
- How can I take care of my health and diet?
- Mental and emotional well-being: Mindfulness, seeking therapy, engaging in social activities, and positive relationships.
- Am I ready to take 100 percent responsibility for my actions which can lead to positive shifts in mindset?

This is the Beginning...

Through my involvement with the Federation of Indian Women Entrepreneurs, I tirelessly advocated for the entitlements rightfully due to women entrepreneurs within the government's purview. The crux of the matter lies in creating an enabling environment for women, a cause that I passionately championed. Our pursuit for a brief stint of single-window registration for women entrepreneurs faced a temporary loss of attention but remained a resilient focus of our endeavors. Over the years, the battle for marketing support for women was hard-fought, culminating in a sizable victory — today, 3 percent of the 25 percent reservation for MSME is exclusively allocated for women entrepreneurs in all government procurements.

The transformative impact of digitization has ushered in an era where doors are swinging open for women entrepreneurs like never before. In the current era, women are remarkably contributing to the entrepreneurial domain, particularly in small businesses. The seismic shift brought about by the modern era is unmistakable, not just globally but prominently within the vibrant entrepreneurial scene in India. The paradigm has evolved drastically. Now you can witness a flourishing community of emerging and distinguished women entrepreneurs. Families, with a notable shift in perception, have acknowledged the undeniable truth that women have equivalent potential as their male counterparts. Bolstered by specific policies geared towards women's empowerment, women have unequivocally proven their ability to form a triumphant league.

May my story serve as a spark that kindles the flames of inspiration and empowerment within you. I wish to remind you that no dream is beyond reach, no challenge is insurmountable, and no path is too treacherous. Each woman carries within her an uncharted ocean of potential.

It is my fervent hope that this book leaves an indelible imprint on your soul, fanning the courage to embrace the unknown. Proudly wear your authenticity, and persist with rock-steady resolve. The folder of my experiences is proof that true greatness lies not in circumventing failure but in the resilience to rise from it and grow.

To my fellow women entrepreneurs, I affirm: the world craves your voice, your vision, and your tenacity. While the disparities may seem substantial, the possibilities are even greater. Let us unite to dismantle barriers, redefine our story, and pave the way for future generations of women.

As you conclude the final pages of this book, remember this is just the beginning; the onset of your phenomenal milestones. Every step you take, every dream you pursue, and every fear you conquer contributes to the legacy of women entrepreneurs preceding you. You are not merely shaping your destiny; you are in the process of transforming the world.

Step forward with courage and conviction, acknowledging that within you resides the power to make a radical difference — not just in your life but in the lives of countless others. Cherish the caravan, for it is within the odyssey that we find our purpose, our passion, and our truest selves.

May this book be a guiding light, a wellspring of inspiration, and a constant reminder that you are not alone. As you venture forth into the world of entrepreneurship, let your light radiate brightly, leaving behind a trail of empowerment that ignites the flames of possibility in the hearts of those who follow.

Always remember, my fellow entrepreneur, your journey is extraordinary, and this is merely the beginning. Relish it. Own it. Change the world with it.

I eagerly anticipate sharing my next book with you as the entrepreneurial landscape continues to evolve in the coming years.

With boundless hope and unflagging faith, I wholeheartedly believe in you.

– Dr. Rajni Aggarwal

Acknowledgments

I owe an infinite debt of gratitude to my wonderful parents, for they have consistently stood by me, unflagging in their support for every endeavor I have pursued. Their guidance has been my foundation, teaching me to be as resolute as a steadfast rock when the world's tempests raged against me, as adaptable as the flowing waters, effortlessly molding myself to any situation that arose, and igniting within me the burning determination to create from the void, forging the person I have become today.

My deepest thanks to my loving husband, Praveen, for his unsolicited encouragement and for always being the person I could turn to during those grueling years of my life. His presence as my confidant made all the difference, and for that, I am eternally thankful.

I am deeply appreciative of my son, Amit, for being my most discerning critic, urging me to introspect and evaluate every facet of my life, which drives me to continuously strive to become the best version of myself. I am also grateful to my daughter-in-law, Pooja, for her warm-heartedness; she has been an invaluable pillar in my journey.

My earnest gratitude to my daughter, Rupali, for being the spring of strength throughout, without whom this book would not have seen the light of day. Her unflinching belief in me has been a driving force. I am equally thankful to my son-in-law, Sunil, for his incredible thoughtfulness and infectious humor, which helped me ease into life.

My wholehearted appreciation to my little army, starting with my only rock star, my granddaughter Meher, and the tiny angels- Shivansh, whose chirping, tantrums, shrieks, and laughter are like sweet music to my soul and Arjun, whose countless kisses and boundless love are beyond measure.

A very special thanks goes out to my dearest friend, Stuti Kacker, who stood steadfastly by my side through all the struggles and successes in my life. Her support has been a beacon of light.

I am also thankful to all those who became catalysts in my life, creating triggers that helped me grow stronger and become the person I am today.

A heartfelt thank you to my brilliant editor, Nitin Dutta, whose keen insights, thorough attention to detail, and committed belief in this project helped shape it into its best possible form.

My gratefulness to all my friends and interviewees who graciously shared their expertise, experiences, and perspectives. Their willingness to impart their wisdom and engage in meaningful discussions has greatly enriched this book, making it a more comprehensive and authentic reflection of the subject matter. Their contributions have been invaluable, and I am profoundly grateful for their kindness.

Most importantly, my deepest gratitude goes to the Almighty, my Guruji, for His perpetual presence in my life. His guidance and influence on my thoughts and actions have been a constant source of strength and wisdom.

References

1. Women Entrepreneurship in India
    http://www.ripublication.com/gjmbs_spl/gjmbsv3n10_15.pdf

2. Why your business' ambiance is key to your success
    https://www.forwardline.com/blog/why-your-business-ambiance-is key-to-your-success/

3. *https://scroll.in/article/680435/flashback-1982-the-asian-games-that-transformed-delhi*

4. *Source: https://www.statista.com/statistics/503249/most-popular-clothing-retailers-germany/*

5. https://economictimes.indiatimes.com/markets/stocks/news/international-womens-day-how-financial-literacy-can-empower-women-in-india/articleshow/98494289.cms?utm_source=contentofinterest&utm_medium=text&utm_campaign=cppst

6. Lending to women entrepreneurs not same as men
    https://www.financialexpress.com/industry/sme/cafe-sme/msme-fin-women-entrepreneurs-business-loan-for-women-credit-for-women-business-p2p-lending-online-lending-digital-lending/1807301/'

7. https://www.statista.com/outlook/335/119/crowdfunding/india@Invest India

8. Apply Business Loan for Women Online – Check Eligibility
    https://www.paisabazaar.com/business-loan/five-leading-business-loan-options-for-women-entrepreneurs/Rahul Mishra from paise Bazar.com

9. You can learn more about who the angel investors are and why they are called Angels From the website: https://hyderabadangels.in/blogs/an-entrepreneurs-guide-to-get-angel-investment-networks-in-india/

10. *How Long Time It Takes To Raise Capital For A Startup.* *https://www.forbes.com/sites/alejandrocremades/2019/01/03/how-long-it-takes-to-raise-capital-for-a-startup/*

11. *https://alejandrocremades.com/*

12. *Albany Office - Legal Aid Society of Northeastern New York.* *https://www.lasnny.org/location/albany-office/* Reference- Between Motherhood and Career - The Hindu. https://www.thehindu.com/opinion/open-page/between-motherhood-and-career/article23936760.ece

13. *Source:https://www.thehindu.com/opinion/open-page/between-motherhood-and-career/article23936760.ece*

About the Author

Dr. Rajni Aggarwal, an internationally acclaimed women's economic empowerment activist, and a first-generation entrepreneur, has spent over four decades of her life in creating several successful ventures.

The first woman entrepreneur to enter hardcore electronics industry back in 1980, she has been the recipient of several awards; National Award winner for 'An Outstanding Entrepreneur' from the Government of India, 1988: 'Leading Women Entrepreneurs of the World Award' from the National Association of Business Women Owners and the Star Group of the United States, 1997; Lifetime Achievement Award' from the Greece Business Women's Association, 2014 and many others.

With a distinguished career spanning decades, Dr. Aggarwal has emerged as a key influencer and leader in empowering women entrepreneurs in India. Founder and President of the Federation of Indian Women Entrepreneurs (FIWE), she has created a powerful launching pad, touching the lives of more than 150,000 women. She represents businesswomen on several governmental boards, such as Trade Committee of Ministry of Industry and Commerce, Pre-budget sessions by Ministry of Finance, and as a Member of the Standing Advisory Committee on Credit Flow to MSME by RBI.

She has traveled extensively worldwide to more than 40 countries and was invited to speak on 'Women Entrepreneurs and the Way Forward at the OECD forum as the Secretary General of the International Federation of Women Entrepreneurs (IFWE) which is as the international arm of FIWE.

Dr. Rajni continues to dedicate her life towards enabling women entrepreneurship in India and endures with the belief; "The meaning of life is to find your gift. The purpose of life is to give it away".

Let's Connect

As we come to the end of this book, I want to express my deepest gratitude for joining me on this phenomenal safari. Your support and engagement mean the world to me.

Our connection does not have to end here. Let us continue this dialogue beyond the pages of this book. I invite you to stay connected through social media, where we can share thoughts, insights, and inspiration.

Here are my social media handles:

Facebook: https://www.facebook.com/rajni. aggarwal.54379

LinkedIn: https://www.linkedin.com/in/fiweglobal/

Email: rajnipk@yahoo.co.in

Thank you for being a part of this adventure. I look forward to staying connected and sharing more experiences in the future.

Milton Keynes UK
Ingram Content Group UK Ltd.
UKHW040439031224
452051UK00005B/26

9 798895 884577